# Marxism in the Contemporary West

**Also of Interest**

*Perspectives for Change in Communist Societies*, edited by
Teresa Rakowska-Harmstone

*The Soviet Union in World Politics*, edited by Kurt London

*The Persistence of Freedom: The Sociological Implications
of Polish Student Theater*, Jeffrey C. Goldfarb

*Innovation in Communist Systems*, edited by Andrew Gyorgy and
James A. Kuhlman

*History of the International: World Socialism 1943-1968*,
Julius Braunthal

*Communism and Political Systems in Western Europe*, edited by
David E. Albright

*The Euro-American System: Economic and Political Relations
Between North America and Western Europe*, edited by Ernst-Otto
Czempiel and Dankwart A. Rustow

*The Continuing Struggle for Democracy in Latin America*, edited
by Howard J. Wiarda

*Brazil: A Political Analysis*, Peter Flynn

*Argentina's Foreign Policies*, Edward S. Milenky

*The Politics of Chile, a Socio-Geographical Assessment*,
César Caviedes

*An Infantile Disorder? The Crisis and Decline of the New
Left*, Nigel Young

*The Spanish Political System: Franco's Legacy*, E. Ramón Arango

# A Westview Special Study

*Marxism in the Contemporary West*
edited by
Charles F. Elliott and Carl A. Linden

What is the relationship between Marxist ideology and the politics of the contemporary West? The contributors to this book treat this question expansively, examining Marxism and the activities of European and Latin American communist parties in the broad context of contemporary Western politics. Their discussion encompasses not only political and practical dimensions, but also addresses important philosophical and moral questions deriving from the clash of Western and Marxist values.

Charles F. Elliott is associate professor of political science and international affairs and chairman of the Soviet and East European Studies Program at George Washington University. Carl A. Linden is associate professor of political science and international affairs at George Washington University.

# Marxism in the Contemporary West

edited by Charles F. Elliott
and Carl A. Linden

LONDON AND NEW YORK

First published 1980 by Westview Press, Inc.

Published 2018 by Routledge
52 Vanderbilt Avenue, New York, NY 10017
2 Park Square, Milton Park, Abingdon, Oxon OX14 4RN

*Routledge is an imprint of the Taylor & Francis Group, an informa business*

Copyright © 1980 Taylor & Francis

All rights reserved. No part of this book may be reprinted or reproduced or utilised in any form or by any electronic, mechanical, or other means, now known or hereafter invented, including photocopying and recording, or in any information storage or retrieval system, without permission in writing from the publishers.

Notice:
Product or corporate names may be trademarks or registered trademarks, and are used only for identification and explanation without intent to infringe.

```
Library of Congress Cataloging in Publication Data
Main entry under title:
Marxism in the contemporary West.
   (A Westview special study)
   Based on a conference held in April 1979 at the Institute for Sino-Soviet
Studies of George Washington University.
   Bibliography:  p.
   1. Communism--1945-     --Addresses, essays, lectures.  I. Elliott,
Charles F.  II. Linden, Carl A.
HX44.M355                  335.43'09045              80-18570
```

ISBN 13: 978-0-367-02172-6 (hbk)

ISBN 13: 978-0-367-17159-9 (pbk)

*To the First Three Directors*
*of the Institute for Sino-Soviet Studies*

Kurt L. London (Director, 1969-1972)
Franz Michael (Director, 1972-1979)
Gaston J. Sigur (Director, 1979- )

# Contents

Preface. . . . . . . . . . . . . . . . . . . . . . . . . . *xi*

1. Marxism in the Contemporary West,
   *Carl A. Linden.* . . . . . . . . . . . . . . . . . . 1

2. Marxism in Latin America,
   *Paul E. Sigmund* . . . . . . . . . . . . . . . . . 20

3. The Four Faces of Eurocommunism,
   *Joan Barth Urban* . . . . . . . . . . . . . . . . 36

4. The PCI, Leninism, and
   Democratic Politics in Italy,
   *Sharon L. Wolchik* . . . . . . . . . . . . . . . . 60

5. Ideology and Organization in the
   Spanish Communist Party,
   *Eusebio M. Muhal-Léon* . . . . . . . . . . . . . 84

6. "Les Nouveaux Philosophes" and
   Marxism, *Michael J. Sodaro.* . . . . . . . . . . 123

7. Freedom, Marxism, and Modern Man:
   Solzhenitsyn's Moral Critique,
   *Charles F. Elliott.* . . . . . . . . . . . . . . . . 149

The Contributors. . . . . . . . . . . . . . . . . . . . *172*
Index . . . . . . . . . . . . . . . . . . . . . . . . . . *173*

# Preface

This volume grew out of a conference on "Marxism in the Contemporary West," held in April 1979 at the Institute for Sino-Soviet Studies of George Washington University. The conference examined the current political expressions of the on-going challenge that revolutionary Marxism and the communist movement pose to today's Western-style democratic civil order. Special attention was given to the "Eurocommunist" phenomenon in its various contemporary shapes as well as to its near relatives. The contributors to this volume treat the subject expansively rather than narrowly. They analyze Eurocommunist-type political strategies of communist parties in the West not only in terms of their broad relation to Marxist and Leninist ideology but also to Western politics and its democratic ethos as a whole. The adaptations of the first in the search for political power are seen in dynamic interaction with the latter two elements. Thus the volume comes to grips not only with the immediately political and practical but with ideological and cultural dimensions as well. It does not, however, attempt a country-by-country survey, but rather, investigates in some depth certain key issues arising from the subject matter. Also, two contemporary schools of critical interpretation of Marxism, the "new philosophes" in France and Solzhenitsyn, are included. The first is indigenous to the West and comes out of a recent chapter of its radical politics and the second provides a view from "outside" the West itself. The volume does not treat the notion of "the West" in any narrow geographic sense but as comprehending countries and societies linked with the modern democratic civil tradition that lies at the core of the term's meaning.

The editors of this volume also wish to express their appreciation to the Institute for Sino-Soviet Studies and its director, Dr. Gaston J. Sigur, for helping to make this volume possible.

*Charles F. Elliott*
*Carl A. Linden*

# 1
# Marxism in the Contemporary West

*Carl A. Linden*

Revolutionary Marxism, it is often observed, has in its history contradicted its founder's theory of modern revolution. Marxism, principally in its Leninist incarnation, has had its most visible successes in capturing power not in the industrially advanced nations of the democratic West as Marx theorized, but in the economically under-developed nations of what is now loosely termed the "Third World." For Marx, a developed Western Europe not only was to serve as the fulcrum of his hoped-for world revolution, but also provide the industrial foundation of his envisioned communist society.

In modern Western Europe social democratic parties shed their Marxism and sought power not on a wave of revolution but through popular election. Finding the path to the seats of authority and the possibilities of major social reform open in Western civic culture, they dispensed with Marxist notions of forceful and total revolution and accepted the constraints of non-violent civil contest. Western communist parties, discovering few openings for revolutionary takeovers in the second half of the twentieth century, began diluting without discarding their Leninist and Marxist articles of faith and adopted electoral alliance strategies for obtaining power. This shift in doctrine and strategy, though varied in form and specific content in the individual Western communist parties, acquired the common name of "Eurocommunism." It amounted to a concerted attempt by such parties to erase the long-time scandal of the failure of Marxist revolution in the Western world. These strategies of Eurocommunism, while attaining some local and temporary successes, have nowhere gained a decisive and enduring victory.

1

In fact, at the beginning of the eighties the chances of such victory for any Eurocommunist party have somewhat dimmed, at least for the time, and the Marxian paradox of success in the Third World and failure in the Western world remains. The Eurocommunist movement, however, continues its energetic effort to find a winning combination in Western electoral politics.

Lenin, who saw a great betrayal of the Marxist faith in the Western social democratic movement, was quick to sense the paradox in the original Marxian prognosis. Not very long after his Marxist faction seized power in Russia in 1917, he gave up his hope and expectation that Western Europe with its large and experienced labor movement, especially in Germany, would generate and sustain a world-wide communist revolution. He turned, it will be recalled, to the idea that communist-led revolution in the East would first have to prepare the way for revolution in the West. The Marxian paradox has applied not only to the "West" taken in a narrow geographic sense. Neither has revolutionary Marxism succeeded in winning power in nations outside the North Atlantic region which have undergone a fair degree of "Westernization" and where Western civil and democratic principles have gained a foothold in their political life.

The paradox does not, however, justify the conclusion that Western or Westernized nations are impervious to revolutionary Marxism under any circumstances. To fasten upon such a conclusion neglects the neither marginal nor inconsequential influence Marxist ideology and Marxist-inspired movements have exerted in the West over the course of modern political history. Contemporary Eurocommunism and its counter-parts elsewhere have built their hopes and programs on this basis and have at least been able to come within striking distance of the seats of governing power on several occasions. Italy provides the foremost example in Europe and the brief rule of Allende in Chile has provided the one case of actual, though short-lived, victory through electoral means.

Marxism as a political ideology, indeed, is broader and more far-ranging than its Leninist version which has historically animated the activity of the various communist parties of the Western world. The activity and influence of such parties cannot be understood in isolation but only in relation to Marxism as a persisting and peculiar ideological, as well as political presence in the

politics of the Western world. Neither can such an
understanding be complete without a consideration of
the relation of Marxist ideology to the democratic
civil ethos and the potentials for crisis and change
in the contemporary West.

Marxism, as an ideology, casts a wide net and
provides at hand a convenient common language of
discourse for those whose discontent with the Western civil order and political tradition is radical
or deep-seated. For some, the language and its pre-
suppositions are adopted wittingly, either in whole
or in part. For many more, it is accepted at least
partially as a plausible and convenient view of the
ways of the world and as a basis for action in the
world.

Indeed, the historical rise of Marxist parties
to dominion and rule in Eastern, rather than Western, lands has produced an impression that Marxism
is more an "Eastern" than "Western" ideology, despite the fact that it arose out of Western philosophical culture. That impression, however, has
been reinforced by various political figures and
writers. Guy Mollet, the former French Premier and
socialist leader, for example, distilled a widespread opinion in his quip that the French communist
party was not "Left" but "East"--its heart was in
Moscow rather than Paris. The late Mao Tse-tung
also promoted the notion of the Eastern-ness of
Marxism with his slogans that the "East is Red" and
the "East wind will prevail over the West wind"
despite the obvious fact that "Red," ideologically
speaking, was originally a Western export.

To say that Marxism arose out of Western culture of course can be understood in two ways--as an
ideology that is a legitimate offspring of that culture or as one that comes out of that culture in
the sense of standing outside of and over and
against that from which it comes. Hence, the question is often asked: does Marxism represent a culmination of or a rupture of Western civic culture?
Marx believed he could have it both ways; his pre-
dicted communist revolution destroys Western class
society, its various forms of political rule and its
intrinsic injustice, on the one hand, and, on the
other, realizes the promise of freedom and equality
in social life which originally arose in the West.
Nonetheless, the notion of a rupture with the civil
heritage of the West is of the essence in the
revolutionary Marx. It prevails over the theme of
continuity that is also found in his thought. The

3

communist revolution, for Marx, could only be built on the foundations provided by the developed Western industrial societies. These foundations which Marx saw as more than narrowly economic and technological constitute the basic element of continuity in his revolutionary doctrine. Nonetheless, the revolutionary process he outlined entails a fundamental, not superficial, change of regime and a break with all past and present political orders that have come forth in Western civic culture.

Marx, like many 19th century Western revolutionists despite his dark picture of injustice and dehumanizing conditions of the industrial society of his time, was, in the last analysis, an optimist and true believer in the idea of progress. He did not heed, for example, the didactic pessimism of the founder of Western political thought, Plato. This father of Western philosophy warned of the strong tendency in man's political affairs to go from bad to worse, and took into account the temptations to which even the best in human nature is peculiarly prone. Modern constitutional thought--including the American--takes this warning seriously and seeks to hedge against the danger in its structuring of democratic institutions. Marx rather thought things in the modern world were getting worse in order, in turn, to get better. He thus offered his well-known five-stage progressive but dialectical ascent to the best regime,* i.e., matured communist society. The contrast of Marx's scheme to Plato's retrogressive but also dialectical five-stage descent in his Republic from the philosophical best to the palpably despotic worst regime is too pointed to be accidental.

Plato warned that tyranny is the final outcome of a process of first losing sight of the right principle of rule and then losing a grip on any principle of rule whatever. He argued that the reformation of politics begins by establishing the right principle of rule in ourselves through reasoning with ourselves and others and thus making self-rule the seed-bed for the best political life.

---

*"Regime" here is used in its general sense of the overall ordering of man's life in association in a specific way.

4

Marx, by contrast, sought the revolutionary over-throw of all principles of political rulership as the precondition of the post-revolutionary communist regime. Only then, he believed, would men enjoy self-rule without political constraints.

Indeed, there may be reason to suspect that Marx put the cart before the horse. Plato's fore-sight rather than Marx's prognostication is borne out by the practice as against the theory of modern Marxist movements which have come to power in the modern world. The calculated destruction of poli-tics that Marxism has sought, and that is in fact realized most categorically in its various Leninist incarnations, has, in practice, resulted in the for-mation of totalist ideocratic despotisms. Communist power structures systematically suppress normal po-litical life in the societies they dominate. These despotic orders ironically allow none to rule them-selves according to their judgment and reason, but impose by force and indoctrination their ideological dictates upon their subjects.

However, the argument is frequently made that despotic tendencies are not inherent in revolution-ary Marxism, especially if it were to come to power in Western or in Westernized societies. Typically, such an argument gains public currency when the electoral strength of communist parties attain for-midable levels through coalitions with socialist or other left-wing parties and they thus gain a chance of attaining governing power by constitution-al or politically legitimate means. In the seven-ties the Eurocommunist current among the communist parties tirelessly promoted this argument. Euro-communist leaders and their circles of sympathizers—whether in Italy, France, Spain or elsewhere--convey the notion that the manifest unfreedom in the domin-ions of their Eastern brethren would not be repro-duced in the West if they were to gain power. Under Eurocommunist rule, they imply, the West would not lose its cultural identity or its democratic soul. Eurocommunism--despite the relative newness of the term--is not unique; Allende in Chile was among its earlier counter-parts.

Characteristically, the Eurocommunist-style leadership focuses on the element of continuity in Marxist doctrine. It plays down the other element of the same doctrine--the notion of a revolutionary rupture with the past. It discounts and sometimes revises those Leninist tenets which both in theory and practice provide justification for revolutionary violence, systematic suppression of opposition, and terroristic methods against the "class" enemy.

Finally, it offers itself as an heir of Western culture, respectful of the rules of democracy and civil rights as well as of the constraints on political action imposed by parliamentary and constitutional traditions.

Many in the Western world have anguished a good deal in recent years over this proferred proposition. It also became a sore point of public debate. Some in the left and others even in the moderate left of center urged that this potentially irreversible experiment in Eurocommunist participation in government be tried. They suggested that in this way Western communist parties might finally become domesticated to Western democratic ways and even sever their long time tie with Marxist-Leninist revolutionism. Such notions recently lost some of their topicality as the fortunes of electoral Eurocommunism declined at the end of the seventies in various Western countries such as Italy, France and Spain.

Further, such notions have tended to lose force in the face of doubts among electorates and Western political elites on Eurocommunism's proclaimed fidelity to the democratic process. Similarly, Allende-ism in republican Chile even more dramatically foundered against these same doubts. Eurocommunism could not easily erase the awareness in the Western world of the chameleon-like character of revolutionary Marxism in its past adaptions to its political surroundings. It has shown Machiavellian skill in relying on craft and the manipulation of appearances as much as main force in the pursuit of power. It proceeds on the premise that not only are men easily deceived but are so because they are first of all ready to deceive themselves. Men also are distracted from the lessons of experience under forceful persuasion, and proceeding on such assumptions, it is ever persistent in the search for a winning strategy and is not fazed by failure. This remarkable persistence in devising strategies, however, is a distinguishing characteristic of communist parties and is rooted in Marxism-Leninism's ideological conviction in ultimate victory. Despite the revisionism of the Eurocommunist party leaders, their typical tracts observe certain political and ideological limits on the policy of adaptation to Western political orders. They do not, for example, renounce Leninism outright. Rather, their revisions focus on specific Leninist formulations. Moreover, such revisions are usually measured, circumspect and qualified lest they lose their identities as leaders of a communist party in the Marxist-Leninist tradition and thus become indistinguishable in ideological line, if not in organizational character from their moderate social democratic and socialist rivals.

The limits of adaptation of Eurocommunist leadership and their counterparts elsewhere to the norms and rules of Western-style democracy is perhaps nowhere more apparent than in their own intra-organizational practice. All Eurocommunist-style leaderships more or less assiduously protect the key Leninist concept of "democratic centralism" against fundamental challenge. The gist of the concept lies in its strict prohibition of "factions"-- i.e., no groupings within the party can openly canvass for and organize support to challenge or unseat the incumbent leadership. Here, of course, the extreme Stalinist and Leninist versions of the concept must be distinguished. The Stalinist version which radically stifles internal debate or expression of differing opinions inside the party organization is rejected and Lenin's version adopted which permitted a measure of internal debate and expression of differences of view--i.e., as long as critics of the party line did not act in concert in promoting their views. Nonetheless, even the Leninist concept remains an extremely effective weapon in the hands of an incumbent leader to ward off and, if necessary, purge challengers. It also well nigh prevents any movement "from below" to change the leadership. A striking example of its usefulness in helping an incumbent leader impose his will is provided in the case of the Spanish communist party's leader, Santiago Carrillo. "Democratic centralism" enabled him to impose his "Eurocommunist" views on the Spanish party despite the reluctance of important segments of the party to accept them. Thus, Carrillo used the same means that enabled his orthodox Leninist counterpart in Portugal, Cunhal, to enforce his views within the Portuguese communist party, sometime earlier.*

---

*See Chapter 5, by Eusebio Mujal-León.

None of this denies strains and conflicts that the flexible Eurocommunist-style political line has produced within communist parties and especially between these parties and the Soviet communist party. Nonetheless, the Leninist organizational practice of Eurocommunist leaders does not harmonize well with their pledges of devotion to the democratic spirit and the legitimacy of loyal opposition. Of course, from the Soviet viewpoint, Eurocommunist selective tampering with Leninist tenets is profoundly questionable. It views as dangerous heterodoxy Eurocommunist assertions that the "dictatorship of the proletariat"--signifying the employment of political violence against opposition--is not the only means to power, but that various electoral coalition strategies with other parties are justified as a means to power in European parliamentary systems. Moreover, in Soviet eyes, the relative tolerance of differing opinions within Eurocommunist parties, for example in today's Italian communist party, undermines party discipline. Such tolerance, the Soviets warn, leads to the self-destruction of the party as a communist party. For the Soviets, the object lesson is provided by the liberalization of the Czech party in 1968 prior to the military intervention to crush that liberalization movement.

Despite the strain in the ties between the Soviet party and the West European parties under Eurocommunist leaderships, such ties still run deep and have, by no means, been destroyed. To cut the cord of connection with the Soviet party and in effect the 1917 Leninist revolution entirely, removes the ground of historical legitimacy from the Western communist parties. Moreover, the claim to be part of a single historically-based revolutionary movement is undercut and their peculiar identity, both ideological and organizational, as communist and not socialist or social democratic parties, is erased. Indeed, to the Soviets' great displeasure, the Italian and Spanish Eurocommunist leaders have blurred and de-emphasized these connections. Yet, ambiguity remains. The ties that bind have not been irrevocably broken.*

---

*See Chapters 3 and 4 by Joan Urban and Sharon Wolchik.

However, what may be more telling is not the unprecedented flexibility of the political lines of the Eurocommunist-type leadership, but rather the unrelenting persistence and constancy of Western communist parties over more than six decades in seeking a successful strategy for attaining power. The Eurocommunist strategies are the latest, and perhaps most daring, phase of a movement that has always been characterized by its combination of opportunism in means and single-mindedness in the pursuit of power. At the core of Soviet-Eurocommunist disagreements is not the goal of revolution, but rather the relationship between the two sides of standard party strategy--the opportunistic side carried to excess can dilute the party's sense of purpose and the doctrinaire side, if too narrowly insisted upon, can close out new possibilities for the seizure of power.

As engineers of revolution, their argument is really about how to mark out and then occupy the ideological and organizational space necessary for a successful bid for power within a democratic civil order.* Indeed, this is what Eurocommunism and its variants outside of Western Europe seek to do. It is for this reason that they question the adequacy of certain classical Leninist formulations for taking power and come into collision with the orthodox line of the Brezhnev leadership in Moscow. However, there is nothing unalterable in the Soviet position. A narrowing of differences with Western parties is always possible, though not, at the present stage, likely. The seed-bed for today's Eurocommunism is, in fact, found in the revisions of Leninist doctrine that occurred in the Soviet party after Stalin's death. Such themes as the permissibility of "different paths of socialism," and the possibility of "peaceful transition to socialism" were incorporated into the Soviet line under Khrushchev's aegis. These revisions of Leninist dogma were characterized as "creative Leninism," i.e., as consistent with Lenin's own revisions of doctrinal formulas to adapt them to changed political circumstances. While the Soviet leadership returned to a more orthodox stand after Khrushchev's fall, and soft-pedaled such changes in doctrine, the revised formulas have not been renounced. Such formulas can

---

*See Chapter 2 by Paul Sigmund.

again serve as a future basis of a more flexible Soviet party line whenever the leadership may deem it to its advantage. While the long symbiosis between the Soviet party and the Western communist parties has become less intimate with the rise of the Eurocommunist tendency, it is still far from dissolving.

In any case, doubt is justified whether revolutionary Marxism in the West, even in its quasi-revisionary forms, can consider the rules of the democratic process as something more than a means to power or method of domination. The Marxist view of man and society rejects most of the philosophical or metaphysical principles which variously and ultimately underlie the popular consensus of the Western democratic civil order. Though such principles are indeed diversely derived in the secular-pluralist societies of the Western world, they nonetheless provide the ground for the broad practical agreement on such central normative concepts as the rule of law, civil liberty and civil rights. Crucial to this diversely constituted consensus is, of course, the common notion that human rights are not a grant of government or society to the individual but rather are the precondition of legitimacy of any rule. While Eurocommunist politicians may and do find the public observance of such concepts of rights and freedom expedient and even necessary under Western conditions, they are not accepted on any basic theoretical grounds found in Marxist doctrine itself. Marx rejects such a view and sees human freedom only as an ultimate outcome of revolution at the end of a long process of development. The ethical and moral relativism of Marxism and its view of the individual human personality as a social product rather than as a being, possessing in some sense an absolute value, disposes the Marxist to regard contemporary democratic civil order as a phase of historical development and thus, in the last analysis, dispensable. In short, any acceptance of the democratic process in Marxism is necessarily conditional, not fundamental.

Marxist doctrine, both in its original and Leninist versions, further sees democracy as one of the political forms of class domination destined to be superceded by a post-revolutionary society free of political or class rule. Marxists are disposed to define democracy in the limited sense of the rule or, more precisely, the domination of the majority over the minority. This is quite apparent in the inner-party doctrine of democratic centralism cited earlier, which is a device for enforcing the majority will, or what passes for it, on the minority. Democracy, more broadly, is not a term normally employed by Marxists to signify a form of rule which presupposes the restraints that a rule of law and democratic civility places on a legitimately constituted governing majority. The rule of law and civility are regarded as illusory while the reality is the domination of society by one or another class-faction. It is indeed on such a basis that Marxism has theoretically equated the "dictatorship of the proletariat" and "democracy" as the domination of a majority class of proletarians over the minority class of capitalists. Under this definition, the latter have no rights to seek to win a majority and thus the right to rule in turn. The Marxist doctrine on democracy means, then, that the ruling power belongs to the stronger. Not included is any necessary stipulation that the majority is not free to take advantage of the weaker, i.e. the minority.

It is not a marginal but an essential and fixed idea of Marxism that a communist party is an agent of an irreversible historical process ending in a permanent and total revolution in human society. This idea militates against the democratic principle that the holders of governing power must yield it up whenever the electoral consensus requires it. The communist party leadership that seeks both to sustain its Marxist-Leninist basis yet to present itself as responsible to a constituted democratic or parliamentary order not only is in contradiction with itself ideologically, but can also find itself at cross-purposes in practice.

In practice, the European Eurocommunist leaderships do seek to repeat the Allende experiment--or something closely resembling it, of course, without suffering its sudden failure. They also seem to have taken from the failure of that experiment one principal lesson, namely, that the social bulwark of democratic civil orders, the middle-class, especially its educated leadership, must not be alienated but either persuaded to accept or at least induced to acquiesece in the entrance of communists into the sphere of governing power.

The case of Allende in Chile whose leadership fitted the latter description is suggestive and lends credence to the classical Leninist view that revolutionary Marxism in the last analysis can only maintain power once won by reliance upon extra-legal force. The only alternative entails a revision of

11

doctrine in which fidelity to the law-regulated democratic principle overrules dedication to the revolutionary principle whenever the two conflict in practice. This is none other than the fundamental revision advocated by the German labor leader Edward Bernstein, at the end of the last century, and Lenin's ideological nemesis. It was out of this revision, first implicitly accepted and then openly asserted, that the moderate social democratic and socialist parties of today's Western and Westernized world arose.

It is this revision which Eurocommunist leaderships stop short of adopting clearly and distinctly. For to embrace it means cutting all the traces of Leninism and a severance of the Soviet connection. It also would mean a shift from the central emphasis of classical Marxism itself. At most, it would seem, Eurocommunism represents not a fundamental revision, but an equivocation of Leninism and Marxism. Whether the equivocation is producing or has already produced an evolution which will eventuate in a change in the heart and mind of Eurocommunism is arguable.*

However, concentration on the enigmas of Eurocommunism and its kin elsewhere can obscure the more basic issue for Western civil culture itself. The critical question is not so much whether or not Eurocommunism represents a latter-day domestication of revolutionary Marxism. Rather, it is even more important to ask how these new configurations in political Marxism are related to the contemporary predicaments of the Western and Westernized world, and what do they signify and portend for the Western type civil order?

These new versions of Marxism can be seen as ideological offerings aimed at assisting Western democracy in an unwitting work of self-destruction gradually rather than suddenly. Or, psychologically speaking, Marxism offers itself as a fulfillment of a kind of death wish inside the Western democratic psyche, or at least as a form of temptation offered to it to succumb and submit to another regime of life.

*In contrast to the main argument presented in this introduction, the chapters by Joan Urban (p. 36) and Sharon Wolchik (p. 60) provide a basis for the inference that, in the case of the Italian communist party, at least, the line between equivocation and evolution may have been crossed and that an evolution is now taking place.

12

Indeed, classically Marxism makes no bones about this aspect of its ideology. It announces itself as the executioner of a degenerating civilization. From this slant, Eurocommunism and its related varieties promise euthanasia rather than a painful and violent death for the Western civil order. Thus, Eurocommunism and its counter-parts have muted the idea of a forceful rupture of the present civil order.

It is perhaps no accident that the latter theme of classical Marxism has been picked up with a vengeance by the numerous extreme left-wing radical groups, which in recent years have resorted to systematic political terrorism in the West. Their Marxist ideology, in fact, centers on the notion of the total destruction of the existing order, subscribing rather literally to Marx's assertion that "force is the mid-wife of history." Their attack on Western democratic leaderships and civil institutions is direct and uncompromising. They seem to operate on the premise that if such leaderships and institutions show themselves incapable of effectual self-defense, they will self-destruct. They are buoyed to their terrorist exploits on the passionate denunciatory rhetoric of Marxism. However, such terrorist Marxist groups have sought their recruits principally among disaffected younger individuals seeking a life-absorbing cause which promises world change.

The pull Marxist ideology has exerted on the radically inclined among the younger generation, principally among university students, may have weakened in the seventies. One notable sign that this may be the case is the phenomenon of the "new philosophers" in France. These intellectual offspring of the radical ferment among French youth in 1968 who accepted Marxism as an ideology of liberation now denounce it as the seed-bed of totalitarian despotism. Not inconsequential in their de-conversion from Marxism has been the impact of the works of Solzhenitsyn, especially his <u>Gulag Archipelago</u>, and the writings of the Soviet dissident movement. While a few of the "new philosophers" have regained an appreciation of Western civic culture, most remain radicals at heart, but now without an ideological homeland to give substance to their faith in world change. They remain in something of an ideological limbo between East and West.*

---

*See Chapter 6 by Michael Sodaro.

In any case, the combination of terrorism and Marxist ideology mentioned above attracts a not numerous and ultra-sectarian strain of radicalized Western intellectuals. Further, where Marxist terrorist groups believe the Western civil order will only disintegrate under a rain of blows from "outside" its own internal political processes, Eurocommunism proceeds on the premise that that order can be transformed from within itself. Its appeal by contrast is aimed at the main body of the adult electorate promising an ultimate relief from contemporary ills without a destructive upheaval. It seeks to strike responsive chords in the Western popular psyche in its search for power. At the same time, it strives to turn educated opinion away from hostility to acceptance of the notion of a compromise arrangement.

While the two strategies are in sharp contrast, their goal is similar. They both seek to convert certain vulnerabilities and potentialities of the Western-type democratic civil order, whether parliamentary or republican, into levers or agencies of a fundamental change of regime. The presence of such potentialities are manifest in the ebb and flow over the years of the electoral fortunes of communist parties in Western Europe, most notably in Italy and France.

The condition of opportunity for challenging the civil order of Western-style parliamentary and republican regimes lies in the characteristic defect of the democratic ethos. Its freedom can turn to license and license toward anarchy. Its egalitarian spirit carried to an extreme corrodes virtually any principle of authority or of command. Under its impact, even the idea of a democratic unity expressed in the motto "from many one" (e pluribus unum) suffers degradation to a pluralistic self-fragmentation. The specific prescriptions of Marxism for curing these defects of the democratic order may change,but its promised treatment is broadly the same; namely, to fill the void produced by democratic disorder and correct the loss of inner direction by replacing democratic pluralism with a monocratic rule. At the same time, its strategy and its rhetoric exploit extreme democratic sentiments as agents of the destruction of the reasoned democratic self-control which make democratic civil orders viable. Those sentiments are aroused and focused against the perennial adversary of egalitarian democracy, namely, oligarchic wealth (i.e., what Marxism calls "capitalism") as a transgressor against economic and social justice. Simultaneously, however, an attack on democratic pluralism and individualism is prepared from behind. The revolutionary regime Marxism seeks to install is totalist and not pluralist.

While Marxism indeed exploits the symptoms of democratic disorder, it does not create them. It is not new wisdom that recognizes that the democratic civil order is prone to certain disintegrative tendencies peculiar to its own nature. These have been especially manifest in the contemporary West in the last two decades or so.

What these tendencies are can only be broadly indicated here, and, while variously definable, they are nonetheless generally familiar. For example, the notion of the popular welfare as central goal of a democratic order can degenerate into an excessive and self-interested consumerism. The pursuit of material satisfactions in turn leads to various degrees and forms of unrestrained hedonism reflected in such phenonema as the rise of an addictive "drug culture" and pornography. Such trends threaten a demoralization of the mainstream culture of the West.

The democratic idea of general progress presuming a measure of current sacrifice for later benefits also can decline into demands for immediate results and a refusal to delay the satisfaction of immediate wants for longer-term needs.

The idea that the human personality is in an essential sense prior to the political community--a principle of modern Western democracy and a basis for its doctrine of political and civil rights--is degraded into a rejection of ties with the larger political community. Citizens turn away from the notion of participation in a general public good and give their prime loyalties not to the larger political society but to narrower associations and special interest groups. Some simply retire into various forms of private self-absorption. Even the widespread notion among democratic individualists that enlightened self-interest requires service to the larger community tends to suffer a slide into the contrary, a thinly veiled assertion of the supremacy of self-interest.

Along with such tendencies a parallel fall in public ethical and private moral standards seems to insinuate itself. The public consensus that democratic civility depends on a common base of citizen virtues tends to be replaced by a pervasive ethical relativism among various groups within society and, in the extreme, by various species of ethical nihilism. The outcome of this tendency, when unchecked, is a widespread ethical and moral solipsism of the present moment which corrodes the social and political relationships holding the civic culture together.

Influential theories in the contemporary West of pressure-group democracy and of the pluralist system --not inappropriately termed "polyarchy"*--unfortunately offer little in the way of antidotes for the above-mentioned tendencies.

These theories together with the widely-shared democratic-egalitarian ideology prevailing in the Western world are hard put to find within themselves a firm ground for democratic authority. Democratic leaderships discover that the traditional basis for effective discipline among themselves and an adequate command over the citizenry to treat or remedy democratic ills has narrowed. The linkages between leaders and led are weakened and, in turn, contribute to a loss of cohesion and even alienation among the principal groups within society. Electorates begin to doubt the ability of democratic leaderships of the center or center-left and center-right to lead and govern in hard tests. Western communist parties have sought to exploit this situation. The Italian party, for example, was entirely explicit in recent years in offering itself as an effective and disciplined substitute for Italy's inefficient and often indecisive democratic leadership. While the disintegrative tendencies that commonly afflict a democratic civil order are neither inexorable or irreversible, the greater their force, the greater the adverse effect on civic morale and the civil order's capacity to resist political challenge.

The challengers to Western civic culture on the left assert that the vices and defects to which that culture is prone, rather than the virtues and humane principles on which it is founded, are identical with its essence. Thus, they typically prescribe a cure for its ills by a radical surgery which strikes at the sources of that order's life. The political surgeons of such an operation will assuredly pronounce it a success, even though the patient does not survive the operation.

Indeed, the domestic political and electoral forces the Western communist parties and the Marxist left have marshalled have never constituted more than a minority element in Western civic culture. It, however, has not been therefore without significance

---

*A term given currency by the contemporary American theorist of democratic pluralism Robert Dahl.

and has frequently wielded influence out of proportion to its size. At times, especially in the 70's, it has enjoyed spurts of growth and the potential for gaining power through coalition strategy was present at various junctures. The ebb and flow of the indigenous challenge of European communism and Marxism in contemporary Western politics is intimately linked with that culture's contemporary strengths and weaknesses. It serves as a kind of measure of its state of health and vitality.

If contemporary Western civic culture suffered demise, it would likely be the outcome of the combined effects of internal and external agencies. Nonetheless, a culture usually opens itself to mortal challenge through its own doing. Vulnerability to attack grows out of the deformation or distortion of its own vital principles. Today the danger arises from the principle of pluralism, the natural twin of democracy. When carried to an extreme it undermines the democratic consensus and in turn the governing authority which rests upon it. The ultimate result is a wearing away of the political unity necessary for the protection of the culture when under challenge.

Eurocommunism seeks a basic change of regime through the systematic and persistent exploitation of democratic pluralism, especially as it is expressed in Western electoral processes. It seeks by electoral alliances to detach enough of the democratic body politic from itself to lift itself into power. The aim of this strategy is not a limited term of rule but the winning of hegemony over the whole body politic to transform it as a whole. If its means are equivocal in the tradition of past Marxist-Leninist practice, its aim of transformation is not. This is the bottom line of today's varieties of Eurocommunism, whether or not its strategy proves workable over time. If in the pursuit of its strategy, it loses its Leninist and then Marxist perspectives, it will no longer be Eurocommunism but a left-wing reformism within the fold of Western civic culture. It then will have been transformed by what it set out to transform. Such ironies of human conflict do and can occur, though it has not happened to any Eurocommunist leadership or its kin so far.

The latter outcome indeed would mark a peaceful conquest of the would-be conqueror by Western civic culture. However, it is not likely to take place unless that culture musters sufficient inner strength to discourage expectation that it can be divided against itself and be overcome. Only then is it possible that the challenger, whose own persistent purposefulness is not at all negligible, might over time undergo an inner change of allegiance.

If excessive pluralism opens Western civic culture to fractional internal division and mortal danger, its own best political wisdom has well understood this characteristic flaw of its ethos--a flaw common to human nature. That wisdom has been given its modern expression by diverse political figures and thinkers. It is found in the American founders' counsel to the people to view themselves candidly in devising forms of self-rule that take into account their own vices as well as virtues; in Lincoln's view of government of, by, and for the people, not as a historical inevitability but a possibility being tested in men's souls; in Tocqueville's insight that, while liberty and equality are twins, an extreme of one destroys the other; and in the Churchillian quip that democracy is a bad form of government but the others are worse.

Behind such examples that come ready-to-mind, there is a broad-gauged civil philosophy which informs Western civic culture. The contributors to that philosophy are legion and span the Judaic, Greek, Roman, Medieval, and Modern periods of Western history. It is a philosophy which, above all, is not a totalistic ideology with an encompassing solution for the ills of man and society as Marxism represents itself to be. It rather has grown out of reflection on the varied experience and practice of more than two millenia of the Western world. It has sought to draw guiding principles out of the political trials of Western man rather than arrive at all-comprehending conclusions about Western history. It has learned to be wary of radical cures for social and human defects likely to prove worse than the disease. With persistence it has sought a salutary compromise between individual freedom and voluntary association, on the one hand, and a lawfully constituted governing authority resting on consent on the other--the first seen as essential to any genuine civil life and the latter as essential to securing the common good of the larger community. That compromise, in turn, has rested on a first premise; namely, that the human being possesses an inherent dignity. This dignity, the Western civil philosophy holds, is manifested in each human being's powers of moral choice and self-determination. Furthermore, these human powers, this philosophy insists, must be held in respect by those who rule and

18

which, when well and freely used, make man's "pursuit of happiness" something more than the pursuit of a Utopian chimera. Here the premise of an inherent human dignity, which is deeply rooted in the Judeo-Christian sources of Western civic culture, most decisively clashes with the Marxist and communist view of things. The premise, which Western civic culture asserts, is not subject to an all-pervading historical relativism; instead it is meta-historical. Modern human history is relative to it, and not the other way round. It is a discoverable truth about human beings which human association must recognize and preserve in its foundations and defend against its nay-sayers. Consciousness of its presence can wane and even be forgotten, but it can also be recovered. It is a truth then which is <u>not</u> a mere creature of time, place, and circumstances, but a truth which measures man himself.*

Indeed, this premise is, in turn, the bottom line of contemporary Western civic culture. It came into view in the course of man's striving to escape despotism and arbitrary rule and to realize political liberty and self-rule. Western civic culture, however, has never been free from the threat of a loss of its identity and a falling back into despotism. The complex and many-faceted challenge of modern Marxism and communism--especially in its most protean of manifestations, Eurocommunism--tests the civic culture's inner strength and resiliency. The latter has the wisdom of its own past at hand. However, it cannot do without another old and once-valued virtue, civic courage. For without it no philosophy, however wise, can be put into practice. The challenges to contemporary Western civic culture can only be answered by the fortitude of its own defenders in preserving its essential principles. Only then can its future be assured as well as the hope of good it contains for humankind.

---

*The focus in Solzhenitsyn's writings on man's "inner freedom" is of a piece with the above-mentioned founding premise of modern Western civic culture. See Chapter 7 by C. F. Elliott.

# 2
# Marxism in Latin America

*Paul E. Sigmund*

In analyzing the influence of Marxism in Latin America, a striking contrast immediately becomes apparent between the organizational weakness of Marxist parties and movements and the pervasive strength of the ideological influence of aspects of Marxist theory, especially in Lenin's theory of imperialism and the economic interpretation of history. This paper will attempt to explain this seeming paradox. Our analysis will survey the history of the communist parties in Latin America since their establishment in the 1920's, trace the organizational and ideological impact of the Cuban Revolution in the 1960's, and evaluate the recent trends in Latin American thought and practice, in order to explain both the theoretical appeal and the organizational failure of Marxism. The explanation that we will attempt to develop relates these phenomena to certain aspects of the Marxist diagnosis of the nature of the problem--and the inapplicability of the Marxist solution--a revolutionary vanguard party based on the dictatorship of the proletariat, and supported by the Soviet Union.

## MARXIST PARTIES

The major communist parties of Latin America were founded in the early or middle 1920's. In Chile, Argentina, and Uruguay, socialist parties had been created before World War I; but the triumph of the Bolshevik Revolution led to splits in the Argentine and Uruguayan parties with those who favored affiliation with the Comintern establishing a small breakaway communist party in each of the two countries in 1920. In Chile, where the Socialist Workers Party dominated a relatively strong labor movement, the party did not split but reorganized itself

as the Communist Party of Chile in 1921-22, and the
Chilean Workers' Federation formally joined the Communist Labor Union International in the latter year.
The Communist Party of Brazil was also founded in
1922 and managed to attract a number of radicals who
had previously supported anarchism.  In Cuba, the
Communist Party had its original base in the University of Havana, although from its establishment in
1925 it attempted to increase its support among
workers.  In Mexico, the Communist Party of Mexico
had been established in 1919 by an Indian, M.N. Roy.
It had some influence on intellectuals and peasant
organizations; but when the Mexican leaders resolved
to create an official revolutionary party, the an-
cestor of the present ruling Institutionalized Revolutionary Party (PRI), and to link the peasantry and
labor organically to that party, it was clear that
the Communist influence in key areas was to be ex-
cluded or at least minimized.[1]

The relative success of the Communist Party in
Chile and its lack of success elsewhere can be explained in two ways.  On the one hand, where the
party was weak, as in Argentina and Mexico, it was
identified as foreign in inspiration and personnel;
and it adhered closely to the Soviet international
line.  Where it was stronger, as in Chile, it already had an authentic national base and tradition
in a pre-existing party and was supported by a strong
trade union movement among coal, copper, and nitrate
miners.  In most of the other Latin American countries in the 1920's, there was little potential for
a trade union base, since industrialization was just
beginning and the proletariat did not exist.

The inapplicability of classical Marxism to
Latin American conditions was recognized at that time
by two Peruvian writers, one who identified himself
as a Marxist, and the other who consciously developed
an alternative to it.  José Carlos Mariátegui was a
founder of the Peruvian Communist Party and wrote a
work called Defensa de Marxismo.  Yet his influential
Seven Interpretive Essays on Peruvian Reality, originally published in 1928, recognized that Peru had no
genuine industrial proletariat and identified the
fundamental problems of the nation as the concentration of land ownership in the latifundia system and
the destruction of the organic Indian society by the
Spanish conqueror.  A fellow Peruvian, Victor Raúl
Haya de la Torre, claimed at the outset to be a
Marxist but argued that while imperialism was the
last stage of capitalism in Europe, in "Indoamerica"
--as he called Latin America--it was capitalism's

21

first stage and would lead to the creation of a new proletariat upon which the revolution could be based. Haya de la Torre founded his own party, the Popular Revolutionary Alliance of the Americas (APRA), originally intending it to be a continent-wide revolutionary movement. Instead, it has become one of the most important parties in Peru, successfully organizing under Haya's leadership a large segment of the workers and a part of the peasantry, fiercely opposing the Peruvian Communist Party and calling for a populist alliance of workers, peasants, and middle classes against foreign imperialism and domestic oligarchy.[2]

The Aprista phenomenon in a way typified the problem for the communist parties in Latin America. Initially the Communists lacked a natural constituency in the labor movement; and when it developed, it was organized by other groups with broader support, a middle-class base, and a nationalist appeal. This is what happened in Mexico with the PRI, in Venezuela with the rise of Acción Democratica (some of the early leaders of which also originally identified with Marxism), and later in Brazil and Argentina, with the organization of labor by the populist caudillos, Getulio Vargas and Juan Domingo Peron. In each case, the "organizational space" offered by the emergence of labor and the ideological space offered by the development of nationalism were taken over by populist rather than Marxist parties and leaders.[3]

In the 1930's, recognizing their own weakness, and reflecting Moscow's decisions on international policy, the Latin American communist parties attempted to break out of their organizational and ideological isolation by cooperating with the middle class and populist parties through the Popular Front. They supported Lazaro Cardenas in his program of social and economic reform in Mexico, cooperated with Batista in Cuba in the 1930's and early 1940's in exchange for his assistance in organizing labor, and in Chile joined the Frente Popular with the middle-class Radical Party and the Socialist Party, helping to elect a Radical as president in 1938. In connection with its participation in the Popular Front, the Communist Party also first developed the doctrine of the via pacifica, arguing that in a democratic system it was not necessary to resort to violent revolution in order for socialism to triumph.

The policy of alliance with middle-class parties enabled the party to extend its influence and organizational efforts in Chile, Cuba, Mexico, and Uruguay, from the mid-1930's until the end of World War II.

With the development of the cold war, however, communist parties fell on hard times. They were persecuted in Mexico after World War II and outlawed in Brazil in 1947, in Chile in 1948, and in Cuba in 1953. Combined with the internal repression and suspicion associated with the last part of Stalin's life, the parties' troubles resulted in a decline of their influence and organizational strength to their lowest point since the 1920's. The one exception was in Guatemala, but the brief period of influence of the Guatemalan Labor (Communist) Party under the government of Jacobo Arbenz was abruptly ended when a CIA-assisted invasion led to his overthrow in 1954. Marxism was identified with communism, communism with the Soviet Union, and the communist parties were seen as agents of a hostile and aggressive foreign power.

All this changed with the advent of Fidel Castro to power in Cuba in 1959 and his adoption of Marxism during the next two years. Starting from an identification with many of the positions of the populist Ortodoxo Party, Castro took an increasingly radical position until finally in December 1961 he announced, "I am a Marxist-Leninist, and I will be one until the last day of my life."[4] Now an authentic Latin American revolutionary embraced Marxism, resisting U.S. efforts to overthrow him and began to take an active role in extending Marxist revolution to the rest of Latin America. Between 1960 and 1968, Castro gave support to guerrilla movements in many parts of Latin America, including not only arms shipments and organizational assistance but actual direct involvement of small numbers of Cuban guerrilla fighters, the most notable of whom was Che Guevara in Bolivia in 1966-67.

With the emergence of Castroism as an important force in Latin America, we must shift our focus from an exclusive concentration upon the orthodox Moscow-oriented communist parties in Latin America. Just as the emerging schism between China and the Soviet Union was leading to the establishment of Maoist parties in Chile, Brazil, and Peru, a new ideological and organizational center, Havana, emerged, headed by a recent convert to Marxism with no particular loyalties to the old communists--who indeed had opposed him until six months before his victory in 1959. During the 1960's, Castroite movements, often under the name Movement of the Revolutionary Left (Movimiento de la Izquierda Revolucionaria--MIR), developed in many Latin American countries and identified themselves with the Cuban Revolution. In the

23

mid-sixties at the high point of the export of the Cuban model, Castro engaged in a public polemic with the orthodox communist parties of Latin America, arguing that the guerrilla revolutionary, even if he is initially ignorant of Marxist theory, is a more authentic Marxist than the party theoreticians who take no action to promote the revolution. The polemic even extended to the Soviet Union when Castro denounced Soviet econmic aid to the government of Colombia and organized his own international organization, the Latin American Solidarity Organization (OLAS), which attacked the Venezuelan Communist Party and condemned "certain socialist countries" for giving credits to "oligarchical governments" in Latin America. The unsuccessful guerrilla movements in the countryside in Peru, Bolivia, Venezuela, Colombia, and Guatemala were succeeded by urban guerrilla organizations in Uruguay, Chile, and Brazil that also claimed inspiration from the Cuban example.[5]

In the sixties, therefore, while Latin American Marxism emerged for a second time from its isolated position and broadened its appeal, it also developed deep internal divisions between orthodox Moscow-oriented parties, those who looked to China for guidance and support and those who were aided and encouraged by Havana. The effects of the split were lessened when Castro effectively ended his support for guerrilla movements in Latin America following the death of Guevara in late 1967 and began to take a less critical line towards the Soviet Union, supporting, for example, the 1968 Soviet intervention in Czechoslovakia. After 1970, Cuban dependence upon, and imitation of, the Soviet Union became even more apparent when, with the failure of the effort to achieve a ten-million-ton sugar harvest, Castro began to institutionalize the Cuban economy and polity along Soviet lines.

Yet an ideological split between the more cautious and pragmatic Soviet-oriented communist parties, and the activist violence-prone radical left of the MIR variety remained. The split was evident within Salvador Allende's Popular Unity governing coalition in Chile between 1970 and 1973. Although himself a member of the Socialist Party, which had been largely Castroite in its orientation in recent years, Allende aligned himself with the Chilean Communist Party's _via pacifica_ in pursuing what he announced in his inaugural address as a "second model of socialism," a _via chilena_ "in democracy, pluralism and liberty," characterized--and here he quoted from Friedrich Engels--by "a peaceful evolution from the

24

old society to the new, where the representatives of the people have all the power and, in accordance with the constitution, can do what they desire when they have the majority of the nation behind them."6 The Socialists and the members of the MIR publicly disagreed with Allende and the Communists on the possibility of a peaceful transition--and one of several reasons for the breakdown of constitutionalism in Chile was the development by the MIR and other radical groups of paramilitary organizations that were viewed as a threat by the Chilean armed forces. Other reasons included a disastrous economic policy that led to a runaway inflation, CIA intervention, and the division of the country along class and party lines, which created a polarized situation which made constitutional democracy impossible. The political polarization was intensified by Allende's statement shortly after coming to power, "I am not president of all Chileans," an expression of his Marxist view of society that drove the members of the relatively large Chilean middle class into fanatical opposition to his regime.

The Chilean intervention was not an isolated event. A similar, although less dramatic, process took place in Uruguay, where the activities of the Marxist urban guerrilla Tupamaro group provoked the armed forces to take more and more power until, finally, civilian rule was destroyed. In 1976 the Argentine military also seized power--overthrowing the government of Isabel Peron and citing inflation and the violence of left-wing guerrilla groups--some of them Peronist, some Marxist in inspiration, and some adhering to a mixture of the two. By the mid-1970's organized Marxism was once more outlawed and persecuted in nearly all the major countries of Latin America. However, the beginnings of a return to constitutionalism were perceptible at the end of the decade, which may permit the legalization of the Marxist parties in a number of countries in the early 1980's.

In contrast to the 1960's, which were dominated by the influence and policy of Fidel Castro, in the 1970's, after an initial period of optimism in Chile, Bolivia, and elsewhere, Marxist parties were persecuted, repressed, and driven underground--and as an organized movement, Latin American Marxism was gravely weakened. The divisions introduced into the movement by the phenomenon of Castroism only made things worse; and indeed, the glorification of revolutionary violence that it involved only accelerated the intervention of those who claimed a monopoly on the legitimate use of violence--the armed forces.

Summarizing, then, a complicated and varied history of fifty years, communist parties and movements have had little success in Latin America for a number of reasons. They were organized before most of Latin America had an important labor movement; and, with the exception of Chile, when labor organizations became established, they were dominated by other parties, mostly of a nationalist and populist orientation. Second, the communist parties were identified as controlled by, and dependent upon, the Soviet Union; and when an authentic Latin American Marxist regime was established in Cuba, it only led to a division of the Marxist left. Third, the communist parties have periodically suffered extreme persecution and repression from Latin American governments. (In the few cases outside of Chile in which they were able to develop a trade union base, it was because they received government support in doing so; e.g., under Cardenas in Mexico in the 1930's and under Batista in Cuba in the early 1940's.) To avoid repression orthodox communist parties have generally downplayed the role of violence in their ideology; but Castroite radical groups of Marxist inspiration contributed to the breakdown of constitutionalism in the 1970's and military intervention in a number of important countries, accompanied by renewed persecution of all those identified with, or suspected of, association with the Marxist left. The orthodox communist parties in such countries as Peru and Chile support a return to constitutionalism, which will provide them with an opportunity to extend their influence. The more radical Marxist revolutionaries are committed to a revolutionary upheaval, such as the Nicaragua revolt against Somoza. Castro, meanwhile, has found that the organizational space that was lacking to him in Latin America is available to him in Africa.

MARXIST IDEOLOGY

The broad appeal of Marxist ideology to many sectors in Latin America stands in marked contrast to the weakness of Marxist parties and organizations. It is not difficult to explain why this is the case. There are many elements in Marxist theory that seem to fit the experience of Latin America. This is most obvious with Lenin's theory of imperialism. To a large degree, Latin American economic development has been carried out under the auspices of foreign investors--first the British, then the Americans, and now the multinational corporation. With, until recently, weak and often corrupt governments which were dependent on the foreign investor for economic survival, it was easy to attribute Latin American economic backwardness to the expansion of foreign influence driven by the needs of the capitalist system. Other ideologies such as populism and Christian democracy could denounce the oligarchy and the foreigner, but Lenin's theory was more detailed in its diagnosis and persuasive in its prescriptions. The foreign presence was motivated by the requirements of mature capitalism for raw materials, markets, and cheap labor; and it required subservient governments and, in many cases, the use of military intervention to maintain its economic power and influence. Wall Street and Pentagon imperialism dominated U.S. policy and determined Latin American economics and politics. The power of U.S. economic interests could explain everything from the landing of the Marines in Central America and the Caribbean in the early part of the century to the overthrow of Allende in 1973. Even the lessening of U.S. influence which was perceptible in the 1970's was attributed to the rise of Brazilian "sub-imperialism" and to the increasing economic importance of capitalist Germany and Japan.

A second and related aspect of Marxism in Latin America is the theory of exploitation. However, instead of deriving their profits from the surplus value produced by the workers in factories of the advanced nations, the capitalists are seen as exploiting the labor of the proletarian nations of the Third World to produce the raw materials and, more recently, cheap manufactured goods on which the advanced capitalist nations depend. The structuralist theory of a non-Marxist, Raúl Prebisch, is adduced here as evidence that the capitalist-dominated world market operates in ways that keep raw material prices down, while continually increasing the price of finished goods that Latin America must import from the more industrialized countries.[7] The boom and bust cycles of international commodity prices and the failure of producers' cartels, except in the area of petroleum, are viewed as further evidence of the exploitative character of international economic relations.

The receptiveness of Latin America to Marxist ideology is promoted by a long tradition of anti-capitalist thinking associated with Catholic and conservative hostility to the cruelties of the market system and support for state intervention to promote social justice. In fact, in Catholic thought

27

in Latin America, it has been possible for Church writers to move very easily from a conservative critique of capitalism to the radicalism of the theology of liberation which identified the capitalist system as the principal obstacle to the attainment of social justice in Latin America.[8] As the development of Peronism demonstrates, it is also easy to move from conservative authoritarianism to a Marxist or radical caudilloism, since both are anti-capitalist, statist, and personalist in nature. When liberal institutions and constitutional democracy have not operated effectively throughout most of Latin American history, the center does not hold; and politics becomes polarized between left and right, which share many of the same characteristics and attitudes.

When traditional institutions are incapable of achieving reform, effective government, or elementary social justice, and constitutional democracy seems unworkable, revolution seems to be the only alternative. Even conservative or moderate parties in Latin America describe themselves as revolutionary; and the myth of revolutionary transformation continues to attract the idealists, intellectuals, and students. Marxism provides a more articulated ideology to give form to the longing for revolution, including a special place for the vanguard, the revolutionary elite that brings the proletariat to recognize its historical role. Latin American intellectuals can see themserves as that elite, even then they reject the party discipline that accompanies the Leninist conception of the vanguard.[9]

Another Latin American attitude upon which Marxism can build is anti-Americanism (or more accurately anti-Yankee feeling, since Latin Americans resent the exclusive appropriation of the term, American, by the United States). While earlier versions of anti-Yankee thinking contrasted the superior qualities of idealism and devotion to spiritual values of Latin America with the materialism and greed of North America, Marxism gives Latin American hostility to "the Colossus of the North" a somewhat different cast. The United States is the center of world capitalism, and anti-Americanism becomes one of a number of cultural and political factors contributing to the widespread distrust and suspicion of capitalism that makes those who harbor these attitudes responsive to Marxist analyses.

There is even a place in Marxist thought for the middle class--although, as noted in the Chilean case, it is difficult to persuade that class that this is the case. At a certain stage of development,

Marxists argue, the national bourgeoisie has a special role in resisting imperialism and advancing national development. This analysis is used to justify alliances with middle-class parties that are viewed as the instruments of that bourgeoisie. Thus, as the Communist Party--but not the other Chilean Marxist groups--understood, a coalition like Allende's Popular Unity could have retained its initial middle class elements, as represented by the Radical Party, and broadened its base in that group by coming to an understanding with the Christian Democrats, without necessarily compromising Marxist ideology. Similarly the peasantry, rejected by Marx as a revolutionary element in his critical remarks about "the idiocy of rural life," has, since Lenin, and certainly since Mao, been recognized as part of a possible revolutionary coalition--indeed in Cuba, the very basis and object of the revolution.

Adam Ulam has argued that there is a "Marxist situation"--a time of instability in the transition from a feudal to a capitalist economy to which Marxism itself was a response when it first occurred and to which it responds again when such a structural situation is repeated. In Latin America there are some evident similarities with nineteenth century Europe as industrialization, urbanization, an increasing birth rate, and rising social awareness produce protests in the name of social justice that can be organized and channeled in a Marxist direction. The contrast between the promise of plenty contained in the expansion of industrialization and economic growth in Latin America and the grinding poverty of the urban and rural masses makes the Marxist explanation of its dialectic causes all the more persuasive.10

While Latin America has been criticized for simply passively reflecting European ideologies, during the 1960's it produced two groups of theories of its own that one might describe as contributions to the development of Marxist thought. First were the theories of revolution based on the Cuban experience and articulated by Che Guevara and Regis Debray. In <u>Guerrilla Warfare, a Method</u> (1963), Guevara argued that it was necessary to establish a mobile but territorially-based rural guerrilla army in order to overthrow the armed forces of the capitalist oppressors. The actions of this army will move through three stages--strategic defense in which surprise attacks gradually wear down the enemy, equilibrium of forces between the guerrillas and the enemy, and, finally, decisive battles, seizure of

29

the cities, and total annihilation of the adversary.
What is Marxist about this analysis? Guevara quotes
from Engels and Lenin on the need to arm the workers,
writes his book in the name of the liberation of the
proletariat, and identifies the enemy as oligarchic
capitalism led by the United States. The vanguard,
however, is not the party--there was no party organization among the Cuban revolutionaries--but the guerrilla army itself. As noted above, this concept of
the guerrilla as the only true Marxist was taken up
by Castro himself in his polemic with the orthodox
parties of Latin America. (The Communist Party of
Cuba was only established in 1965, and it did not
hold its first congress until 1975. Only one or two
of the members of the Popular Socialist Party (PSP)
--the earlier orthodox communist party--hold positions of power in the new party.)

Guevara's theory and Castro's practice were
given another influential formulation in Regis
Debray's Revolution in the Revolution?, published in
1967. Debray argued that insurrectional activity in
the countryside was the first duty of a Marxist revolutionary and criticized the city-based Marxist
politicians who did nothing to aid the revolution.
He saw the party and Marxist consciousness as emerging out of the experience of rural guerrilla warfare
which welds together a guerrilla nucleus (foco) of
workers, peasants, and intellectuals in the face-to-
face confrontation of the people's war. Following
the defeat of Guevara's guerrilla force in Bolivia
and increasing disillusionment with the possibilities
of guerrilla warfare in Latin America, Debray repu-
diated his views; but they remain an important statement of the Castroite modification of Marxist
revolutionary theory.[11]

Castro's Cuba has also made a practical contribution to Marxism. In the mid-1970's, it developed
the concept of "people's power" (poder popular), a
system of competitive indirect elections which has
given the form, if not the substance, of representative government to Cuba. Under this system, two or
more candidates are nominated in each district for
seats in municipal assemblies. Those elected by
majority vote (a runoff election is customary)
choose the municipal executive committee, as well as
delegates to provincial assemblies and to the National Assembly of People's Power, which is the
supreme legislative body and elects the executive.
In October 1976 and April 1979, elections were held
under the new system. Not surprisingly, the National
Assemblies elected on both occasions chose Fidel

30

Castro as chairman of the Council of State and Prime Minister.

A second and more complex contribution to Marxist thought by Latin America in the 1960's was the theory—or better stated, theories—of dependencia. Arising initially as a criticism of Latin American policies of import substitution, the dependency writers emphasized the internal and external constraints on Latin American development that are produced by its involvement in the world capitalist system. Not all of the dependencia writers were Marxists. Osvaldo Sunkel, for one, rejected "inevitable laws or historical tendencies," maintaining that, instead, international economic relations were characterized by "contradictions that create the possibilities for choice and...the manipulation of the variables that are subject to direct influence."[12] Sunkel argued for Latin American economic integration, investment controls, and changes in the system of foreign trade to reduce Latin American dependence. For most of the dependence writers, however, the international capitalist system was the source of the economic forces that were systematically "underdeveloping" Latin America; and a socialist revolution was the only way in which the continent could break out of its dependent situation. Betraying their Marxist orientation, they insisted that as long as Latin America remained a part of the international capitalist system, it would continue to be exploited; and only a fundamental transformation of external and internal political and economic relations could end the system of dependencia.

In the case of the dependencia and other writers, it is often difficult to determine the degree of Marxist influence on Latin American social scientists. All or nearly all such writers use Marxist terminology in their analyses; and the mere fact that a writer refers to accumulation, imperialism, the bourgeoisie, exploitation, or the proletariat does not thereby make him a Marxist. Other elements —the central position of the class struggle, the dialectic of history, the party as the vanguard of the proletariat, and economic determinism—should also be evident in an author's writings before he is identified clearly as a Marxist.

Many of these elements are not present in the writings of contemporary Latin Americans, even those who clearly identify with the left. It is difficult to accept as a vanguard party the petty and divided factions that pass for Marxist parties in Latin

31

America today. The dictatorship of the proletariat is even more difficult to endorse when organized workers are a "labor aristocracy" in Latin America, ranking usually in the upper 25 percent of the population in the distribution of income. A peasantry which is quickly satisfied by distribution of small land plots and that resists the collectivization of agriculture does not look like a revolutionary class. Advocacy of violence which only produces much more intense repression and bloodshed, especially for the lower classes, does not appear to be the way to improve the lot of the poor. Materialist interpretations of reality meet the resistance of a deeply Catholic culture, which holds spiritual and ideal values in high esteem. Proletarian internationalism does not receive a warm response from a continent in which the strongest contemporary ideological force is that of nationalism. The criticisms of contemporary capitalism made by Marxism are widely accepted, but its solutions command much less support.

Where Marxism was successful as in Cuba and, for a time, in Chile, it was able to channel the much stronger forces of Latin American nationalism and populism into a Marxist direction. Castro began as a populist and was always a nationalist--and only after he came to power did he move to Marxism-Leninism. Allende was not a member of the Communist Party but of the more nationalistic Socialists; and his coalition included Catholics, middle-class Radicals, and a variety of non-Marxist groups. The notion, widely prevalent in the U.S. in the early 1960's and still influential in the making of current policy, of a "coming explosion in Latin America," in which Marxist revolution sweeps from the Rio Grande to Tierra del Fuego, is an exaggerated reaction to the Marxist-influenced rhetoric of Latin American intellectuals and students--not a practical judgment of the contemporary organizational potential of Latin American Marxism.

In most Latin American countries, the Communist and Castroite groups have not succeeded in taking on the nationalist and populist characteristics which, it is the argument of this paper, are required for mass support. Where constitutional democratic systems operate, other parties and groups have organized the workers and built coalitions of the middle class, the peasantry, the workers, and the poor. The bulk of the Latin American church does not follow the theology of liberation, which itself differs from Marxism in many important respects (e.g., the role of the party, its attitude towards violence, and the

32

materialist interpretation of history). The state apparatus in most Latin American countries has become larger and stronger in recent decades; and the economies of some Latin American countries; e.g., Brazil, Mexico, Venezuela, and Ecuador are growing rapidly. The armed forces continue to have support in many Latin American countries precisely because they are able to draw on nationalism to legitimate their actions. Marxist rhetoric and political reality are still sharply separated; and, barring a worldwide economic collapse or the rise of a charismatic leftist leader in the confusion following the overthrow of a dictatorial regime, the Marxist parties will continue to be a small but ideologically influential minority on the contemporary Latin American scene. The coming explosion in Latin America may be a long time in coming.

NOTES

1. On the history of communism in Latin America see Robert J. Alexander, Communism in Latin America, New Brunswick, N.J.: Rutgers University Press, 1957; Ronald M. Schneider, Communism in Guatemala, 1944-1954, New York: Praeger, 1959; Rollie E. Poppino, International Communism in Latin America, Glencoe, Ill.: The Free Press, 1964; Karl M. Schmitt, Communism in Mexico, Austin, Texas: University of Texas Press, 1965; Robert J. Alexander, The Communist Party of Venezuela, Stanford: Hoover Institute, 1973; Ronald M. Chilcote, The Brazilian Communist Party, New York: Oxford, 1974; and Luis E. Aguilar (ed.), Marxism in Latin America, rev. ed., Philadelphia: Temple University Press, 1978.
2. See José Carlos Mariátegui, Seven Interpretive Essays on Peruvian Reality, Austin, Texas: University of Texas Press, 1971, and the excerpts from Haya de la Torre's writings, translated by the editor in Paul E. Sigmund (ed.), The Ideologies of the Developing Nations, 2d rev. ed., New York: Praeger Publishers, 1972, pp. 383-398. For analyses of the two writers, see Miguel Jorrin and John D. Martz, Latin American Political Thought and Ideology, Chapel Hill, N.C.: University of North Carolina Press, 1970, pp. 277-280 and 335-357.
3. On "organizational space" and its relation to the efforts of Latin American governments to include new groups in a "support coalition," see Alfred Stepan, The State and Society: Peru in Comparative Perspective, Princeton, N.J.: Princeton University Press, 1978, esp. ch. 3.

4. For Castro's ideological evolution, see the speeches translated in Sigmund, *Ideologies*, pp. 332-367.

5. On the divisions of the Latin American left in the 1960's, see D. Bruce Jackson, *Castro, the Kremlin, and Communism in Latin America*, Baltimore: Johns Hopkins Press, 1969; Richard Gott, *Guerrilla Movements in Latin America*, London: Thomas Nelson, 1970; Donald Herman (ed.), *The Communist Tide in Latin America*, Austin, Texas: University of Texas Press, 1973; and William E. Ratliff, *Castroism and Communism in Latin America*, 1959-1976, Washington, D.C.: American Enterprise Institute for Public Policy Research, 1976. Documents illustrative of the positions of the Cubans and of the orthodox Communists are translated in Paul E. Sigmund (ed.), *Models of Political Change in Latin America*, New York: Praeger Publishers, 1970, pp. 101-114, 250-254. For urban guerrilla ideology, see the excerpt from the writings of Carlos Marighela, translated in Sigmund, *Ideologies*, pp. 470-478.

6. Paul E. Sigmund, *The Overthrow of Allende and the Politics of Chile*, 1964-1976, Pittsburgh: University of Pittsburgh Press, 1977, p. 131.

7. For analyses of Prebisch's thought, see Albert O. Hirschmann (ed.), *Latin American Issues, Essays, and Comments*, New York: Twentieth Century Fund, 1961, pp. 12-23, and a forthcoming book by Joseph Love.

8. See Paul E. Sigmund, "Latin American Catholicism's Opening to the Left," *Review of Politics*, vol. 35, no. 1 (January 1973), pp. 61-76.

9. On the appeal of Marxism to Third World intellectuals, see John Kautsky (ed.), *Political Change in Underdeveloped Countries*, New York: John Wiley, 1962.

10. Adam Ulam, *The Unfinished Revolution*, New York: Random House, 1960. However, for arguments that revolution is unlikely in Latin America, see Claudio Veliz (ed.), *Obstacles to Change in Latin America*, New York: Oxford University Press, 1965, and John Mander, *The Unrevolutionary Society: The Power of Latin American Conservatism*, New York: Knopf, 1969.

11. See Regis Debray, *Revolution in the Revolution?*, New York: Grove Press, 1967, and Debray's retraction of his views in *La Critique des Armes*, Paris: Editions du Seuil, 1974, ch. 5. For Guevara see John Gerassi (ed.), *Venceremos!, The Speeches and Writings of Che Guevara*, New York: Simon and Schuster, 1968.

12. Osvaldo Sunkel, "National Development Policy and External Dependence," in Sigmund, _Ideologies_, p. 442. For examples of Latin American _dependencia_ theory, see Teotonio dos Santos, _Dependencia y Cambio Social_, Santiago: CESO, 1970, and "The Structure of Dependency," _American Economic Review_, vol. 60, no. 2 (1970), pp. 231-235; Fernando Enrique Cardoso, _Dependencia y Desarrollo en America Latina_, Mexico: Siglo XXI, 1969; and Anibal Quijano, "Imperialism and International Relations in Latin America," in Julio Cotler and Richard Fagen (eds.), _Latin America and the United States: The Changing Political Realities_, Stanford, Cal.: Stanford University Press, 1974, pp. 67-91. For good critical reviews of the large _dependencia_ literature, see David Ray, "The Dependency Model of Latin American Development: Three Basic Fallacies," _Journal of Inter-American Studies_, vol. 15, no. 1 (1973), pp. 4-20, and C. Richard Bath and Dilmus D. James, "Dependency Analysis of Latin America," _Latin American Research Review_, vol. XI, no. 3 (1976), pp. 3-58.

# 3
# The Four Faces of Eurocommunism

*Joan Barth Urban*

The second half of the 1970's saw the emergence of Eurocommunism as a pole of attraction and topic of controversy on the already crowded spectrum of European Marxist currents. The term itself, coined in late 1975 by the Yugoslav-born correspondent of a centrist Italian news magazine, was widely adopted by journalists, politicians and academics alike. But the nature of the phenomenon it sought to describe remained elusive. While government spokesmen on both halves of the European continent derided Eurocommunism as a political ruse of the other side, more dispassionate analysts tried to fathom its essential characteristics.[1] Did Eurocommunism mean simply the expedient adaptation of some European Communist parties to the liberal democratic rules of political life in the West? Did it signal a more fundamental shift away from their Leninist, as well as Soviet, origins? Were the three major parties commonly identified as Eurocommunist—the Italian, French and Spanish CP's—so diverse in political program and structure that no single rubric could justifiably be used to categorize them?

In fact the Eurocommunist phenomenom defies simple definition and can best be understood by exploring its multiple facets—what I call the four faces of Eurocommunism. The first is its revisionist face, its acceptance in principle of the value of parliamentary politics and the primacy of national interests. The second is its polycentric face, its support for doctrinal diversity and regional affinity in the building of a socialist society. The third is its loyalist face, its insistence on maintaining a special relationship with other sectors of the world Communist movement, most notably the Soviet Union and its client states in East Europe.

The fourth is its _evangelical_ face, its urge to influence its more orthodox comrades in an innovative direction.

The degree to which these four attributes applied to any one West European CP during the 1970's varied, of course. It can be argued that the French party was more revisionist than polycentric, more loyalist than evangelical, while the Italian and Spanish parties were as much the one as the other.[2] Each party, however, manifested to some extent all four characteristics.

## The Revisionist Face: Reformism and Nationalism

In discussing the revisionist face of Eurocommunism, a distinction must be made between revisionism as a process and Revisionism as an eminent school of thought within the European Marxist movement at the turn of the century. While the history of Marxism may be viewed as one of successive revisions, Revisionism signified the reformist and nationalist orientation that figured so prominently within the Socialist International on the eve of World War One.

The Eurocommunists' accommodation to electoral politics and parliamentary institutions differed little from that advocated by the father of Revisionism, German Social Democratic leader Eduard Bernstein, at the close of the nineteenth century.[3] Nor was such conduct on their part of recent vintage. In the 1930's the French Communist Party (_Parti communiste français_, PCF) had supported a popular front coalition. In the mid-1940's both the PCF and the Italian Communist Party (_Partito comunista italiano_, PCI) had complied with the democratic rules of the game, as evidenced first by their entry in 1944 into coalition cabinets that they could not hope to dominate,[4] and subsequently by their conformity to legal norms even after Cold War polarization led to their exclusion from governmental participation in May 1947. By the mid-1950's it had become commonplace for PCI spokesmen to talk of building socialism gradually through incremental changes, or "structural reforms," brought about by democratic means. Some two decades later the PCF, PCI, and to a lesser extent the reemergent Spanish Communist Party (_Partido Communista de España_, PCE) had once again become prominent contenders for ministerial posts in their respective parliamentary governments. It was in this context that they declared their allegiance to civil liberties, pluralist democracy, and the alternation in power of electoral majorities in a

37

series of much publicized bilateral (1975) and multilateral (1977) statements.[5]

Moreover, just as the early twentieth century social democrats' acceptance of the domestic political order enabled them, in August 1914, to justify their patriotic support for the call to arms, so too the Eurocommunists' gradual accommodation to the domestic political environment led them in due time to concede the primacy of national interests over international commitments. Like any other political party competing in the electoral arena, their postures on foreign policy issues began to reflect broad domestic public sentiments in the 1970's: the Italian Communists supported European integration and acquiesced in NATO membership; the French Communists opposed both, extolling absolute national sovereignty; the Spanish Communists urged Spain's entry into the European Economic Community but not into NATO.

For the Eurocommunists, in short, class-based internationalism receded to a level of secondary importance; and the apocalyptic revolutionary vision of Marx and Lenin was overshadowed in their theoretical perspectives by preoccupation with medium-term, or transitional, strategies.

At first glance the Eurocommunist shift from revolution to reformism bore a certain resemblance to Soviet doctrinal development. Had not Moscow endorsed electoral politics as far back as the popular front days of the 1930's, if only as a way of containing the spread of Fascism? Had not Khrushchev declared at the Twentieth CPSU Congress in 1956 that the utilization of parliamentary methods might pave the way to a peaceful transition to socialism? On closer inspection, however, Soviet ideologues right up through the late 1970's warned against exclusive reliance on peaceful and legal means of revolutionary transformation. In their polemics with the Eurocommunists they ridiculed the idea that the bourgeoisie might quietly relinquish power in the untoward event of a majority vote for socialism.[6] Particularly after the overthrow of Allende's Unidad Popular regime in Chile, they counseled infiltration of the military, the media, and the police in conjunction with the quest for electoral support.[7] (Indeed, it seemed in 1975 that the Portuguese CP had taken a leaf straight from their book in its unsuccessful bid for total power.) In contrast to the Western political establishment, the Soviet leaders doubted not the sincerity but the wisdom of the Eurocommunists' commitment to a legal and democratic transition to socialism.

But even given a legal electoral Communist victory, what was to prevent the new regime from evolving into a tyranny of the majority over the minority, the "dictatorship of the proletariat" envisaged by Marx? The Eurocommunists, for all their talk of evolutionary socialism, had yet to disavow historical determinism—the conception of the inevitability of socialism. Italian and Spanish (not to mention French) CP media and official statements exuded confidence in the inexorable march of history toward socialism. For example, PCI leader Enrico Berlinguer—in his formal report to his party's fifteenth congress in early spring 1979—spoke of "the historical necessity" of the October 1917 Revolution in Russia and of "the relentless transition" from the age of capitalism to the age of socialism.[8] Spanish Communist documents were often couched in similar terms.[9] It was, moreover, not uncommon for individual cadres from both parties to exhibit the superciliousness of those convinced of their insight into the laws of historical development. This was the case despite PCE leader Santiago Carrillo's comment at the 1976 East Berlin Conference of European CP's that the Communist movement was beginning to shed its "mysticism of predestination."[10] It continued to be the case despite the PCI's description (in the draft theses for its fifteenth congress) of the "thought of Marx, Engels, and Lenin" not as an all-inclusive canon but as a "reference point" and "research tool" to be critically verified in relation to reality, experience and other schools of thought.[11]

To the extent that determinism remained an integral part of the Eurocommunists' interpretation of history, the eventuality of ideological and political monism could not be ruled out. If the coming of socialism was assured by the laws of history, and Communists were graced with exclusive knowledge of those laws, what rationale could there be for the observance of democratic principles under socialism? Not surprisingly, this theoretical ambiguity found practical expression in the political arena. The French union de la gauche, whose prospects for winning governmental power had looked so bright in the mid-1970's, went down to electoral defeat in 1978 largely because of the PCF's doctrinal rigidity and political hubris. The French Communist Party sought to impose its programmatic views and to secure essential parity in any future distribution of ministerial portfolios even as

39

minority partner in the alliance with the French Socialists.[12] (During the mid-1970's public opinion polls consistently placed the Socialists well ahead of the Communists, and in the March 1978 National Assembly elections the Socialists won 22.5 percent and PCF 20.5 percent of the votes cast.) What might the PCF have demanded as majority partner, observers wondered.

By way of contrast, the PCI's policy stances were flexible and moderate. Its official spokesmen were also conciliatory toward their Socialist compatriots, even in the face of the harsh polemical campaign launched against the PCI by the Italian Socialist Party (Partito socialista italiano, PSI) in the summer of 1978.[13] Yet it could be argued that the PCI's electoral strength afforded it the luxury of flexibility and tolerance. As the winner of fully three times as many votes as the Socialists in the parliamentary elections of both 1976 and 1979 (the PCI polled upwards of 30 percent and the PSI about 10 percent of the total), the Communists would clearly dominate any potential coalition government of the left. (In this context, it should be noted that the electoral returns of the Spanish Communist Party were comparable to those of the PSI, i.e., about 10 percent, in the parliamentary elections of 1977 and 1979.)

## The Polycentric Face: Pluralism and Regionalism

On a theoretical plane the Italian Communist Party went far in resolving the above-noted contradiction between democracy and determinism by adopting a polycentric view of the historical march toward socialism. During the 1950's and 1960's the notion of polycentrism elicited as much attention from publicists as did the idea of Eurocommunism a decade later. Even the errors in perception were similar in that both were frequently interpreted in strictly geographic terms, whereas the central thrust of each was primarily strategic. The popular understanding of polycentrism was that of the world Communist movement divided into regional sectors. But in its original formulation it also meant the existence of multiple transnational trends toward socialism, variously centered in the Communist, social-democratic, and non-aligned movements. As then PCI leader Palmiro Togliatti said in his celebrated Nuovi argomenti interview of June 1956, with reference to the non-Communist world: "There are countries where we wish to start socialism although the Communists are not the leading party. In still other countries, the march toward socialism is an objective for which there is a concentration of efforts coming from various movements...The whole system becomes polycentric, and even in the Communist movement itself we cannot speak of a single guide."[14]

The concept of polycentrism, if not the term itself, was central to the international orientation and theoretical outlook of post-1948 Yugoslavia. Boycotted by the Soviet bloc and wary of excessive dependence on the Western capitalist powers because of the threat to political cohesion at home, the Titoist leadership was compelled to look elsewhere for ideological reinforcement. This it found at first among the Scandinavian social democrats but later, and more significantly, among the newly independent "progressive nations" of the third world. The upshot was Yugoslav sponsorship of the non-aligned movement as a counterpoise to East-West polarization and superpower pressure. But the prerequisite for a genuine entente of non-aligned states was the renunciation of ideological exclusivism. Marxism-Leninism, Tito-style, remained in force within Yugoslavia. However, as the 1958 <u>Programme of the League of Yugoslav Communists</u> said of the world revolutionary process at large, "The conception that the Communist parties have a monopoly over every aspect of the movement of society towards socialism, and that socialism can only find its representatives in them and move forward through them, is theoretically wrong and in practice very harmful."[15] The Yugoslav program went on to say that Communist parties should instead recognize that socialists in the West and progressive movements in the less developed countries constituted an integral part of the socialist process, and that the CP's must in effect earn the right to a leading role in the overall movement toward socialism. In other words, for the Titoists the theoretical underpinning of non-alignment was a polycentric view of socialist development.

Carried to its logical conclusion, polycentrism on the international level implied pluralism on the domestic level. If Communist, socialist, and third-world progressive forces could acknowledge the legitimacy of one another's contribution to world socialism, it could be argued that diverse political currents might also cooperate in the building of socialism within the confines of a given nation-state. The Titoists were reluctant to concede the validity of this logic for their own country, first for power-political reasons and later (in the 1970's) on the grounds that multi-partyism would exacerbate the ethnic tensions that already threatened the viability of the Yugoslav state. It was therefore left to the innovative leadership of the PCI to translate polycentrism into pluralism.

Palmiro Togliatti—in his above-quoted June 1956 interview—actually coined the term polycentrism to signify the strategic approach discussed above. The growing warmth of PCI relations with the Yugoslav Communists, highlighted by Togliatti's visit to Belgrade in May 1956, suggests that the Italian leader's thinking was influenced by the Titoists' theoretical formulations. Like the Yugoslavs, Togliatti focused on the polycentric nature of international trends toward socialism. At the same time his special concern was with developments in the capitalist West, and this led him to broach the possibility there of a variety of domestic forces working toward socialism. As he said with reference to "countries with highly advanced capitalism..., we cannot rule out that even in these countries, parties which are not Communist but are founded in the working class can express the drive provided by the working class in the march to socialism. Moreover, even where strong Communist parties exist, there can exist at their side other parties which have some roots in the working class and a socialist program. The effort to carry out radical economic changes in the capitalist system, along lines which in general are those of socialism, can also originate, lastly, from movements which are not considered as socialist."[16] Togliatti's comments foreshadowed his party's future endorsement of both pluralism and regionalism.

But conditions were not yet ripe for the articulation of such advanced formulas. The wrenching impact of deStalinization throughout the pan-European Communist movement, the loss of control by party elites and of confidence on the part of militants, drove the Khrushchev regime to reassert doctrinal orthodoxy. As the Hungarian revolution was being put down by armed force, Soviet ideologues laid down a series of "general laws" for the construction of socialism. The ambiguous slogan of "different paths to socialism" that had heralded the post-Stalin easing of Soviet controls over East Europe (and rapprochement with Yugoslavia) now gave way to CPSU insistence on the leading role of the Communist party and the obligatory inculcation of

Marxism-Leninism under socialism.[17] Moscow's imposition of the "general laws" throughout the Soviet bloc and parallel campaign against revisionism as the "main danger" within the international Communist movement all but precluded the idea of socialist pluralism. Soon thereafter the eruption of Sino-Soviet tensions, exacerbated by Peking's initial success in winning the support of a number of Asian CP's, also tainted the regionalist connotation of polycentrism.

Moreover, during the 1960's the Italian center-left formula of a Christian Democratic coalition with the Italian Socialist Party left the PCI isolated, virtually eliminating the political space required for a pluralist strategy on the left. Throughout the post-1956 period the PCI's probes at theoretical innovation were also relentlessly assailed by Moscow and its loyalist allies, including at that time the PCF.[18] The Italian party, in turn, was fairly restrained in its response, at first because of relative electoral weakness (the PCI—like the PCF—polled only somewhat over one-fifth of the popular vote in national elections until its jump from 22 percent to 25 percent in the 1963 parliamentary contest) and later during the center-left era because of the attendant political isolation.

All this changed in the late 1960's. The Soviet Union's armed suppression of the 1968 Prague reform movement brought home even to committed West European Communists the stark reality that the "general laws" were merely a pretext for Moscow's domination of East Europe and similar designs on the world Communist movement at large. The Warsaw Pact invasion of Czechoslovakia thus drove the PCI to distance itself explicitly both from the Soviet model of socialism and from CPSU doctrinal prescriptions, a step long favored by influential sectors of the party intelligentsia and adumbrated by Togliatti as early as 1956. Domestic developments pointed in the same direction. Economic slowdown combined with governmental stasis had the dual effect of discrediting the center-left formula and polarizing the Italian political scene. Trade-union militancy and radical youth activism were accompanied by a surge in terrorism and a resurgence of neo-Fascism. In other words, circumstances both in the European Communist movement and at home were conducive to the PCI's formulation of a new policy for gaining and exercising power: hence the vision of socialist pluralism and the strategy of the historic compromise (compromesso storico).[19]

The following decade saw the fleshing out of the PCI's programmatic commitment to a pluralistic form of socialism and its consequent denial of the very existence of the CPSU's "general laws." In 1969 generic pronouncements to this effect were made both by Luigi Longo, Togliatti's successor as PCI head, and Longo's own heir apparent, Enrico Berlinguer. Inspired in part by the Unidad Popular experiment in Chile, Italian party spokesmen in the early 1970's spelled out the need for Communists and Socialists to compete as well as to collaborate under socialism, deploring the PCI's early postwar goal of ultimate fusion with the PSI.[20] At the Thirteenth PCI Congress in early 1972 the formal political resolution added the Catholic left to those forces that would help to mold the contours of socialism in Italy. During the mid-1970's official party statements alluded frequently to the prospect of multiple political forces competing in a socialist Italy. But the theses prepared for the PCI's 1979 congress were the most precise to date on this point. While acknowledging in proper Marxist fashion the class basis of party politics under capitalism, thesis 12 went on to argue that even after the elimination of antagonistic classes under socialism, "Diverse interests continue to exist, and various intellectual, political, cultural, and religious orientations and traditions retain importance and value. Hence the existence and function of several parties—and of their alternation in government—even during the task of the democratic and socialist renewal of society, and during the task of the building and direction of a new society."[21]

Berlinguer's articulation of the compromesso storico strategy in September 1973 flowed naturally from this programmatic moderation, signifying as it did the readiness of the PCI to cooperate with the centrist Christian Democrats during a transitional stage on the path to socialism. By the same token, the PCI's acquiescence in Italy's NATO membership was a logical corollary of its anticipated accommodation with Christian Democracy. Both policies, in turn, were designed to overcome the political polarization of the early 1970's and to avert a Chilean type scenario as the PCI moved closer to a share in governmental power. Nevertheless, a clear distinction remained between the historic compromise as a strategy of approaching socialism and socialist pluralism as a mode of building socialism. Inherent in the PCI's programmatic projections was the

assumption that at some point the approach to
socialism would coincide with its acceptance by such
an overwhelming majority of the population that
competitive democratic politics would not endanger
the new order.  The capitalist-oriented political
forces of both Catholic and lay inspiration would be
reduced to vestigial rumps.

In short, socialism was still the historically
ordained wave of the future.  But the stipulation of
its concrete shape was no longer proclaimed as the
prerogative of the PCI alone.  The evolution of
transnational polycentrism into socialist pluralism
thus helped to resolve the contradiction between
political democracy and historical determinism.  It
legitimized freedom of political choice even within
the framework of the historical inevitability of
socialism.  It did little, however, to endear its
Italian Communist proponents to the fatherland of
socialism.  If anything, CPSU polemics against the
PCI intensified during the 1970's, the Italian
party's substantial electoral gains notwithstanding.
The reconciliation of democracy and determinism in
theory only threatened further to undermine the
legitimacy of Soviet practice.

As for the regionalist facet of polycentrism,
it had always been inherent in the concept albeit
subordinate in importance to the strategic thrust.
Togliatti and his successors categorically rejected
the idea of regional centers, especially within the
Communist movement where the autonomy of each CP was
hailed as paramount.  Nevertheless, a regional
orientation was implicit in some of Togliatti's
comments in 1956.  And in his famous memorandum
penned in Yalta on the eve of his death in 1964 he
spoke openly of the need for regional CP meetings to
discuss questions of mutual concern.[22]

The alliance that developed between the PCI and
the Spanish Communist Party (PCE) in the late 1960's
finally created the basis for a regional West European CP entente.  Both parties condemned unequivocally the Soviet-led invasion of Czechoslovakia and
the later consolidation of a hardline conservative
regime in Prague.  When Moscow retorted by lending
covert support to pro-Soviet factions in the Spanish
party, the PCI gave political and organizational
backing to the Carrillo leadership.  At the same
time, the Carrillo group embraced the programmatic
goals of political pluralism and a united socialist
West Europe.  Still outlawed in Franco's Spain with
its leaders largely confined to exile, the PCE's
adoption of a line similar to that of the PCI seemed

45

more a calculated gamble than the result of an independent and searching theoretical elaboration over time. But by the time of the PCE's legalization in early 1977, Carrillo had been largely successful in inculcating among his party's cadres a polycentric view of socialism.

It was the Portuguese upheaval of mid-1975 that provided the final impetus for the emergence of the Eurocommunist grouping of Italian, Spanish, and French CP's. At that time the Portuguese Communists under the leadership of Alvaro Cunhal aspired to a minority seizure of power through infiltration, manipulation and intimidation, all techniques that recalled October 1917 as well as the more recent Communist takeovers in postwar East Europe. Just as Moscow's rigid orthodoxy toward Czechoslovakia in 1968 had spurred the PCI (and PCE) to articulate a pluralist alternative to Soviet-style socialism, Portuguese CP extremism likewise impelled the other Latin European CP's to differentiate in some dramatic fashion their own policies from those of Cunhal. Thus in a series of bilateral declarations they proclaimed their commitment to a democratic electoral revolution and a pluralist model of socialism. To be sure, the PCI and PCE moved first, signing a joint declaration in support of democratic principles in July 1975 while their Portuguese comrades were still in the ascendancy in Lisbon. The French party, on the other hand, remained for a time ambivalent as to both Portuguese developments and its own role in French society. Although it had agreed to join the <u>union de la gauche</u> with François Mitterrand's Socialist Party in 1972, it was only during the course of 1975 that the PCF leadership began to endorse (for reasons which are still unclear) "bourgeois" democracy and civil liberties as a matter of principle. It was therefore not until mid-November 1975 that it added its voice to the proponents of socialist pluralism in a joint communiqué with the PCI. But as the year 1975 drew to a close, Eurocommunism as a geographic constellation and programmatic stance distinct from the <u>Portuguese</u> as well as Soviet model had entered the European political arena.

Eurocommunist relations with other sectors of the European left also experienced some spillover from the Portuguese events of 1975. The PCI and PCE not only denounced Cunhal's contempt for democratic norms; they also endorsed the political moderation of the Portuguese Socialist Party of Mario Soares. Thenceforth PCI consultations with Northern European social democratic and labour parties—a process that had begun in 1969 and that included unofficial contacts with the German SPD—multiplied.[23] Some nineteen such parties sent delegates to the Fifteenth PCI Congress in the spring of 1979.[24] It was against the backdrop of these growing contacts that the PCI advanced the idea of a "new internationalism"—in contradistinction to "proletarian internationalism"—during the Soviet-Eurocommunist polemics triggered by the preparations for the June 1976 Berlin Conference of European CP's.[25] Under the rubric of the "new internationalism," the Italian Communists sought through cooperation with European socialists and Catholic and lay progressives, at the trade-union level and in the European Parliament, to advance incrementally the cause of a socialist West Europe. Polycentrism in the sense of a diversity of transnational currents participating in the march toward socialism thus once again became topical.

## The Loyalist Face: "The Ties That Bind"[26]

If Moscow viewed the reformist facet of Eurocommunism with skepticism, it looked upon the nationalist, pluralist, and regionalist facets with trepidation and outright hostility, above all because of the threat they posed to the legitimacy of Soviet-style rule at home and in Eastern Europe. "National Communism" had been taboo at least since the 1948 Stalin-Tito split. From the time of Togliatti's postulation of polycentrism in 1956, CPSU publicists denounced the idea of regional variants of Marxism. They were if anything even more intransigent toward socialist pluralism, equating it at best with crass opportunism and at worst with imperialist subversion. It was thus hardly surprising that "Eurocommunism" was eventually subjected to similar diatribes.

From the mid-1950's through the early 1970's the PCI bore the brunt of Soviet polemics, as befit its position as the standard-bearer of theoretical innovation among the West European CP's. Beginning in 1974, however, Moscow reserved its most cutting and explicit attacks for the Spanish party, probably as much because of the PCE's outspokenness as because of its vulnerability, first as a clandestine and later as a minor domestic force. Here it should be noted that in the early 1970's, PCE leaders began to charge the Soviet Union with a status quo orientation in <u>West</u> Europe as well as East Europe—on top

47

of their criticisms regarding Czechoslovakia and
Soviet domestic repression in general. In 1975 the
French CP added its voice to these accusations,
especially with regard to Soviet ambivalence toward
revolution in the West. CPSU-PCF relations deter-
iorated forthwith but never quite reached the level
of tension that existed between the Soviet and
Spanish parties.

Regardless of the timing and intensity of polemics with Moscow, however, all three Eurocommunist
parties rejected out of hand the idea of a rupture
with the CPSU. In the case of the PCF this was
rather to be expected given the French party's
belated and somewhat ambivalent process of differ-
entiation from the Soviet model. More puzzling was
the PCE's opposition to a break in inter-party ties
despite the CPSU's interference in Spanish factional
disputes as well as public slights and censure of
Carrillo (and others). Most notable was the conciliatory conduct of the PCI. Party leaders not
only repeatedly denied any intention of breaking off
ties with the CPSU; they were also bent on observing
proprieties. Unlike PCF leader Georges Marchais,
Berlinguer attended both the Twenty-fifth CPSU
Congress in 1976 and the sixtieth anniversary cel-
ebration of the October Revolution in 1977. Then in
1978 he journeyed to Moscow for bilateral talks with
Brezhnev. Unlike their Spanish comrades, moreover,
PCI critics of the Soviet system tended to be ab-
stract and academic rather than polemical. Perhaps
because of the Italian party leaders' much longer
history of open disagreements with the CPSU, they
had concluded that reasoned discourse rather than
verbal confrontation was a more effective means of
getting their way vis-à-vis Moscow. But this only
begs the basic question of why they still felt
compelled to take Soviet views and attitudes into
consideration.

The Eurocommunist CPs' insistence on maintaining
ties with the CPSU may be explained by considerations of historical identity, ideological affinity,
and political calculation. With regard to the first
point, each became a significant political force at
a time when it was inextricably linked to the Soviet
party. The PCF became a mass party during the popular front era. Yet the popular front policy was
devised and conferred upon the French CP leadership
by the Comintern oligarchs in Moscow.[27] The PCE, a
minor partner in the initial Spanish popular front
coalition, achieved political saliency only during
the Spanish Civil War, thanks to the material aid

and political advisers dispatched from the Soviet Union in support of the Republican cause. After Franco's victory in 1939, the Spanish CP's clandestine status further enhanced its material and psychological dependence on Moscow. The PCI alone can be said to have won domestic prominence by virtue of its own initiatives. From an outlawed band of some 5,000 militants in 1943 it grew to a mass party of well over one million members by late 1945, partially as a result of Resistance policies that differed in significant respects from those dictated by the CPSU.[26] On the other hand, many of those new recruits rallied to the Communist cause not because of the specifics of the PCI line but because of their awe and admiration for the Red Army's prowess and the presumed wisdom of Josef Stalin—characteristics that they shared with the PCF's wartime adherents. Moreover, long-time leader Togliatti, whom the PCI now hails as one of its greatest theorists, was a top-ranking Comintern official during much of the 1930's. In other words, the Italian, French, and Spanish CP's entered the postwar era firmly rooted in the international Communist matrix—in contrast to the Titoists and Maoists who mobilized their devoted cadres and won their revolutionary victories in isolation from if not defiance of Moscow. Hence a break with the CPSU could entail a far greater blow to their historical identity than was the case with the Yugoslav and Chinese CP's.

Considerable ideological affinity also served to tie the Eurocommunists to the CPSU, despite all the doctrinal divergences that developed in the 1970's. A recurring refrain in their commentaries on the Soviet Union seemed to be, "'existing socialism,' no; October 1917, yes!" Although the PCF still clung to the idea of "general laws," all three parties denied the relevance of "existing socialism" (read Soviet model) to their own societies and increasingly questioned its suitability even to the USSR. Nevertheless, they hailed without reservation the historical significance and legitimacy of the October Revolution. While Bolshevik voluntarism— and violence to democratic principles—could be construed as compatible with historical determinism, it was hardly consistent with the Eurocommunists' latterday defense in principle of a democratic and pluralist revolution. The Western CP's explained away this contradiction with reference to the threat from imperialism and backwardness of Russia in 1917. But in all probability the Russian Revolution constituted an issue wherein ideological affinity and historical identity had become hopelessly intertwined. For the Italian, French, or Spanish CP's to deny the legitimacy of October 1917 would mean to disavow their own legitimacy as well.

On questions relating to the third world, the views of the Eurocommunists and the CPSU also converged. Imperialism was an ever-present and virulent enemy to be combatted by whatever means necessary. Violence in the struggle for national independence or ethnic sovereignty was the norm. And even after victory respect for Western democratic principles was not required. As Carrillo wrote in his famous tract, "Eurocommunism" and the State, "Those who demand pluralist and parliamentary development...for Vietnam, Laos, and other regions of the Third World, where such institutions have never had any historical existence, are baying at the moon."[29] This attitude differed little from the Eurocommunist posture on the Russian Revolution.

It also served a practical function. Commitment to third world liberationism provided an outlet for the ideological militancy and millenarian fervor that was frustrated at home by the Eurocommunists' domestic commitment to a gradualist electoral revolution. Circumstantial evidence for this may be found in the coincidence in timing during 1978 between major PCI statements in support of liberation struggles and the growing malaise among PCI members over their party's ambiguous governmental role. (In effect, by joining Italy's parliamentary majority in March 1978 the PCI had assumed responsibility without power.) As a case in point, Berlinguer's closing speech to the annual September festival of the party daily, l'Unità, created a sensation because of his acclaim for third world liberation movements and ringing tribute to the role of Leninism and the October Revolution in advancing their cause.[30] Clearly he was seeking to reaffirm the PCI's revolutionary credentials in the eyes of its rank-and-file members

Political calculation also played a role in the Eurocommunists' relationship with the CPSU. Here a central element was the presence of pro-Soviet sentiments among elements of the base (as well as the leadership in the case of the PCF) and the danger to party cohesion that a break with Moscow would entail under these circumstances. There were two forms of pro-Sovietism: a residual attachment to the myth of Soviet prowess that had gripped the imagination of militants throughout the Stalin era but especially

50

during the Resistance and early postwar years; and the more cool-headed attachment of unionized working-class activists—the hard-hat generation of the 1950's and 1960's—who were concerned not with the fate of Soviet dissidents but with the material status of Soviet factory workers. The Spanish CP seemed to exhibit primarily the first form, which provided the emotional impetus for the anti-Carrillo factionalism of the late 1960's. Within the French CP both types were fairly widespread. Thoroughly Stalinized by the late 1920's, French Communism was long marked by an almost fanatic devotion to the Soviet homeland and its vozhd. The predominantly working-class character of the PCF leaders and base, their ouvrierisme, reinforced that blind devotion with the more doctrinaire and corporatist, or self-interested, dimension of proletarian camaraderie.

In the case of the Italian CP, on the other hand, the idealized image of Soviet reality that characterized the early postwar generation had faded perceptibly by the 1970's. This was due in part to the fact that important elements of the PCI leadership had never been fully bolshevized,[31] thereby facilitating Togliatti's prompt denunciation of Stalinism after 1956. It was the ouvrieriste variant of pro-Sovietism that was most evident within the PCI. Indeed, among sectors of the party's labor constituency a veritable hard-hat mentality developed during the 1970's. On the one hand, the unionized industrial workers were intent on defending the improvements in wages and working conditions that they had won during the turbulent "hot autumn" of 1969. On the other hand, they were disdainful toward the "disadvantaged" strata of Italian society —the unemployed radicalized youth and the unassimilated southern emarginati encamped around the northern cities. On both accounts they opposed the PCI's official austerity policy, articulated in 1977, that called for curbing industrial wage increases as a means of reducing inflation, improving productivity, and ultimately alleviating unemployment.[32] This hard-hat opposition, in turn, led the party leadership to deplore what it called the "corporatist impulses" that were emerging among working-class elements. As the theses for the 1979 congress put it, "The most serious danger is that of a deterioration in the relationship between the employed and the unemployed...The danger is that within the employed working class...the commitment to represent the general and progressive interests of the country will slacken."[33] The blue-collar workers' opposition to the PCI's austerity policy

51

was accompanied by doubts about the <u>compromesso storico</u> as a whole and, it may be surmised, tacit agreement with Moscow's allegations regarding PCI opportunism.

Given these pro-Soviet attitudes, it stood to reason that the Eurocommunist leaders were reluctant to let tensions with the CPSU reach the breaking point. They feared disaffection if not defection within their ranks and a consequent weakening of their domestic power base. But in addition to considerations of party cohesion, the West European CP strategists doubtless calculated that the maintenance of ties with Moscow could serve a more far-reaching political purpose. Were the PCI or PCF to enter a coalition cabinet, other Western powers might well be deterred from retaliatory measures, in the economic sphere or otherwise, by the threat of Soviet countermoves in support of the country concerned. There was yet another tactical reason for avoiding an open rupture with the CPSU. The opportunity for influencing political evolution within the Soviet orbit depended at least partially on the degree to which channels of inter-party communication remained open.

## The Evangelical Face: The Democratization of "Existing Socialism"

During the second half of the 1970's the Spanish and Italian CP leaderships maintained with ever greater insistence that the realization of the Eurocommunist vision of socialism in West Europe would contribute to the democratization of the Soviet Union and East Europe. To be sure, there were differences in tone and emphasis. Carrillo was more polemical than the PCI <u>leaders</u> (as distinct from Italian party intellectuals who could be as scathing in their depiction of Soviet reality as any Spaniard). Official PCE spokesmen tended to accentuate the negative aspects of the Soviet system while Berlinguer and his associates stressed instead the universal relevance of democratic values. As Berlinguer put it in his closing speech to the 1977 l'Unità festival, the constellation of ideas known as "Eurocommunism" was inspired not by a limited regional perspective (<u>una chiusura regionale</u>) but by "a global historical vision."[34] Still, the thrust was the same. A democratic and pluralist form of socialism in the West would have a contagious impact on the Soviet bloc.

52

1977 was the year in which these views were explicitly articulated. Carrillo's "Eurocommunism" and the State, published in the spring, was notable for his provocative assertion that the Soviet system was not fully socialist because of the absence of democratic institutions. He concluded his essay with the suggestion that the advance of socialism "in the developed capitalist countries" might help to transform the Soviet Union into a "real working people's democracy."[35] During the controversy between the CPSU and PCE that Carrillo's book triggered, the Italian CP staunchly defended the Spanish leader's right to speak his mind. On the substance of the issue, however, key Italian Communists insisted on the socialist nature of the Communist party-states. They then proceeded to argue that "the renewal of existing socialist societies" could best be aided not by polemical criticism but by promoting the victory of Eurocommunism in the "metropoles of capitalism."[36] In plain English, reforms in the East would be stimulated by the example of more attractive forms of socialism in the West.

The Spanish CP presumably put the accent on Soviet repressiveness in an effort to disassociate itself further from the CPSU as Spain moved toward its first free elections of the post-Franco era in June 1977. The Italian party, on the other hand, explained its relative restraint vis-à-vis Moscow by emphasizing the force of example as a potential contribution to the elimination of Soviet repressiveness. The need for explanation stemmed, in turn, from the mounting unrest in East Europe during 1976-1977 and the PCI's own public sympathy for Czech, Polish, and Soviet dissidents. But support for democratic evolution in the Soviet bloc rested on broader considerations. It was the logical corollary of the Eurocommunists' position that socialist pluralism was the form of political order most appropriate to advanced industrial societies.

During the preparations for its fifteenth congress, the PCI formally equated the Eurocommunist program with a "third way" (terza via) of socialist construction, one that would bridge the historic gap created in 1920 between Communism and social democracy while also constituting an improvement upon both. As Berlinguer asserted in his opening address to the congress, the "third way" represented in fact a third phase of socialist development following upon the experience of the Socialist International and the subsequent era ushered in by the October Revolution. Although it "set great store by the

53

previous two phases and critical reflections upon
them," the "third way" of Eurocommunism was an
historically more advanced stage in the world revolutionary process.[37] The congress theses spelled
out what Berlinguer implied: by pursuing this path
the "workers' movement of Western Europe" would be
able decisively to contribute to anti-imperialism,
international peace, and "the democratic development
of existing socialist societies."[38]

To repeat, however, the basic prerequisite for
Eurocommunist influence on the Soviet bloc's evolution toward political moderation was the retention
of reasonably amicable ties between the CP's of East
and West Europe. For only under such conditions
would the Italian and Spanish (and French) CP's be
able to lend encouragement to the more moderate and
innovative elements within the hierarchies of the
Soviet-style regimes (for example, in Poland and
Hungary). And only then would there be some hope
that the polycentric vision of socialism might win
legitimacy on that half of the European continent.

By way of conclusion a brief discussion of the
questions raised at the outset of this essay is in
order. First of all, there is no doubt but that
Eurocommunist reformism had its genesis in expe-
diency. The PCI and PCF first adapted to their
respective liberal democratic environments (with
Moscow's initial blessing) because the alternative
of manning the revolutionary barricades with
weapons garnered from the maquis would have spelled
defeat and possible political extinction. On the
other hand, the subsequent evolution of Eurocommunism, in particular the postulation of strategic
polycentrism, signified a departure from the spirit
if not always the letter of the Western CP's
Leninist and Soviet matrix. For the reasons noted
earlier, the Eurocommunist parties still hailed
Lenin and the October Revolution in the 1970's. Yet
their avowal of a polycentric path to a pluralist
form of socialism was the antithesis of Lenin's
practical works: the Bolshevik Revolution, the new
Soviet state, the Third Communist International.
Finally, the Italian, Spanish, and French CP's were,
strictly speaking, too diverse to permit a common
classification. By the late 1970's the PCF was
clearly reformist and nationalist, but its commitment to pluralism and regionalism remained ambivalent. Its conduct prior to the 1978 National
Assembly elections raised doubts about its pluralist

54

credentials, while its opposition to (in contrast to PCI support for) the expansion of the EEC's membership and powers augured poorly for its contribution to effective coalition politics in the new transnational European Parliament elected in June 1979. The French party leaders were also less outspoken than their Italian and Spanish comrades in their criticism of "existing socialism" and in their expectations regarding Eurocommunist influence on the Soviet bloc. By and large, however, the designation of all three parties as Eurocommunist had as much conceptual validity as the categorization of systems as different as those in Czechoslovakia, Poland, Hungary, and Bulgaria under the single rubric of Soviet-style regimes.

More generally, this essay approached the phenomenon of Eurocommunism from the vantagepoint of what its proponents said more than what they did. It stressed "theory" rather than practice, unavoidably so in many cases because of the Eurocommunists' own concern with programs (socialist pluralism) or policies (transnational coordination within the West European left) not yet realized in practice. It therefore raises questions of plausibility. This is especially the case in view of the widespread assumption that should these parties enter their respective national governments they would behave no differently than the East European CP's after World War Two: in a word, they would seek exclusive power in the service of Soviet interests.

The following considerations point to the alternative possibility that the leaderships of the Italian, Spanish and perhaps even French CP's (viewed from the perspective of mid-1979) would continue to play the democratic game if given positions of governmental responsibility. For the PCE to do otherwise would be highly impolitic given the fact that it commands even less support within the Spanish left than did its Portuguese comrades in 1975. In the case of the much stronger PCI, a bid for total power on the East European pattern would almost certainly lead to an economic boycott by the industrialized Western nations, on whom Italy relies for nearly three-quarters of her foreign trade.[39] Should the PCI manage to retain its grip despite such a boycott, it would most likely be forced into economic dependence on Moscow with all the attendant political consequences. In the final analysis, the Eurocommunists may still feel bound by special ties to the CPSU; but they surely do not care to be subject to the Brezhnev Doctrine! This

55

holds for the PCF as much as for the PCI although France is, to be sure, less geopolitically vulnerable to potential Soviet pressure than is Italy. Policy-makers in all three parties are well aware that the history of postwar East Europe has been one of repeated attempts by Communist party leaders—Tito, Nagy, Hoxha, Ceausescu, Dubcek—to extricate themselves from Soviet domination. They are also aware that when push came to shove, the alternative was either outright rupture (Yugoslavia and Albania) or a Soviet-instigated change in leadership (Hungary and Czechoslovakia). In short, there is some reason to suppose that the Eurocommunist leaders would prefer to seek their political fortune in the context of Western parliamentary politics rather than to risk placing their political careers and respective national power bases in jeopardy.

NOTES

1. For the best analyses of Eurocommunism in English, see Rudolf L. Tökés, ed., Eurocommunism and Détente (New York: New York University Press, 1978); David E. Albright, ed., Communism and Political Systems in Western Europe (Boulder, Colorado: Westview Press, 1979); and William E. Griffith, ed., The European Left: Italy, France, and Spain (Lexington, Mass.: Lexington Books, 1979). My discussion of the Spanish Communist Party is based largely on insights gained from talks with and works by Eusebio M. Mujal-León, who contributed chapters to all three of the above-cited collected volumes.

2. I explore the differences between the French CP, on the one hand, and the Italian and Spanish CP's on the other in my chapter, "The Impact of Eurocommunism on the Socialist Community," in Innovation in Communist Systems, edited by Andrew Gyorgy and James A. Kuhlman (Boulder, Colorado: Westview Press, 1978).

3. One of the best studies of Bernstein's life and thought is by Peter Gay, The Dilemma of Democratic Socialism (New York: Collier Books, 1962).

4. During a two-week period spanning March-April 1944, the PCI and PCF made the decision to accept minor ministerial positions in future coalition cabinets. This step was presumably part of Stalin's larger design to secure Western acquiescence in Soviet hegemony over East Europe.

5. Bilateral PCI-PCE and PCI-PCF statements were signed in July and November 1975 respectively,

and a joint communiqué was endorsed by all three parties in March 1977. For the texts see l'Unità, July 12 and November 18, 1975 and March 4, 1977.

6. For example, see V. Zagladin, "Revoliutsionnaia epokha oktiabria," Pravda, November 6, 1978, pp. 4-5.

7. For the CPSU's reaction to developments in Chile and Portugal, see my "Contemporary Soviet Perspectives on Revolution in the West," Orbis, XIX, 4 (Winter 1976), pp. 1359-1402.

8. L'Unità, March 31, 1979, pp. 9-16 at p. 9.

9. This assertion is based on information provided by Mujal-León.

10. Text in Santiago Carrillo, Escritos sobre Eurocomunismo, Vol. I (Madrid: FORMA ediciones, 1977), p. 104.

11. Progetto di tesi per il XV Congresso nazionale del PCI (Rome: l'Unità DOCUMENTI, 1978), p. 3. For this reason, the theses continued, "we have held for some time that the formula 'Marxism-Leninism' does not express all the richness of our theoretical and intellectual patrimony."

12. For details see Frank L. Wilson, "The French CP's Dilemma," Problems of Communism, XXVII, 4 (July-August 1978), pp. 1-14.

13. Notable in this regard was PSI leader Bettino Craxi's essay in the news weekly Espresso denouncing in thinly veiled terms the PCI's continuing commitment to Leninism, which Craxi equated with unqualified totalitarianism; see "Il Vangelo socialista," l'Espresso, August 27, 1978, pp. 24-29 and 98.

14. English text in The Anti-Stalin Campaign and International Communism, edited by the Russian Institute, Columbia University (New York: Columbia University Press, 1956), pp. 98-139; see p. 139 for the above quotation.

15. The Programme of the League of Yugoslav Communists (Belgrade: Edition JUGOSLAVIJA, 1958), pp. 43-72; see p. 62 for the above quotation.

16. The above quotation is taken from Togliatti's report to the PCI Central Committee of June 24, 1956, the English text of which appears in The Anti-Stalin Campaign, pp. 193-267; see p. 213. The emphasis is mine.

17. Zbigniew Brzezinski, The Soviet Bloc, second revised edition (Cambridge, Mass.: Harvard University Press, 1967), pp. 271-337.

18. See Donald L. M. Blackmer, Unity in Diversity: Italian Communism and the Communist World (Cambridge, Mass.: The M.I.T. Press, 1968); and

François Fejtö, The French Communist Party and the Crisis of International Communism (Cambridge, Mass.: The M.I.T. Press, 1967). passim.

19. For an illuminating analysis of the origins of the compromesso storico, see Stephen Hellman, "The Longest Campaign: Communist Party Strategy and the Elections of 1976," in Italy at the Polls, edited by Howard R. Penniman (Washington, D.C.: American Enterprise Institute for Public Policy Research, 1977). I deal with the emergence of PCI support for socialist pluralism in "Socialist Pluralism in Soviet and Italian Communist Perspective: The Chilean Catalyst," Orbis, XVIII, 2 (Summer 1974), pp. 482-509.

20. Ibid., pp. 486-487.

21. Progetto di tesi per il XV Congresso, p. 2.

22. English text in William E. Griffith, Sino-Soviet Relations, 1964-1965 (Cambridge, Mass.: The M.I.T. Press, 1967), pp. 373-383; the above point is made on p. 374.

23. Angela Stent Yergin, "West Germany's Südpolitik: Social Democrats and Eurocommunism," Orbis, XXIII, 1 (Spring 1979), pp. 51-71; and Heinz Timmermann, "Democratic Socialists, Eurocommunists and the West," in The European Left.

24. Le Monde, March 31, 1979, p.8.

25. For an early discussion of the "new internationalism" see "L'azione internazionale del PCI e la riunione dei comunisti europei," l'Unità, February 14, 1976, p. 13.

26. A more extended discussion of this theme may be found in my chapter, "The Ties That Bind: West European Communism and the Communist States of East Europe," in The European Left.

27. Daniel R. Brower, The New Jacobins: The French Communist Party and the Popular Front (Ithaca, New York: Cornell University Press, 1968), pp. 47-67.

28. Most notably, the PCI agreed to the operational principles of parity and unanimity within the Italian Committees of National Liberation, thereby giving veto power to each constituent party and assuring inter-party compromise in the common (national) interest.

29. Santiago Carrillo, "Eurocommunism" and the State (London: Lawrence and Wishart, 1977), p. 19.

30. L'Unità, September 18, 1978, pp. 2-4.

31. I develop this argument in "Italian Communism and the 'Opportunism of Conciliation,' 1927-1929," Studies in Comparative Communism, VI, 4 (Winter 1973), pp. 362-396.

32. For an excellent survey of the PCI's recent economic policies, see Michael J. Sodaro, "The Italian Communists and the Politics of Austerity: The Dialectics of Deradicalization," MS, Institute for Sino-Soviet Studies, The George Washington University, 1979.

33. Progetto di tesi per il XV Congresso, p. 7.

34. L'Unità, September 19, 1977, pp. 3-4.

35. Carrillo, "Eurocommunism" and the State, p. 172.

36. See, for example, PCI Secretariat member Paolo Bufalini's address to the 1977 l'Unità festival in l'Unità, September 11, 1977, pp. 1 and 17.

37. Ibid., March 31, 1979, p. 10.

38. Progetto di tesi per il XV Congresso, p. 2. Berlinguer made the same point indirectly by reading the following quotation from Lenin: "In the West things will be done differently. We may make mistakes, but we hope that the Western proletariat will correct them. We appeal, therefore, to the European proletariat, begging them to help us in our work." See note 37 above.

39. Robert D. Putnam analyzes Italy's economic interdependence with the West in "Italian Foreign Policy: The Emergent Consensus," Italy at the Polls, and "Interdependence and the Italian Communists," International Organization, XXXII, 2 (Spring 1978), pp. 301-349.

# 4
# The PCI, Leninism, and Democratic Politics in Italy

*Sharon L. Wolchik*

One of the largest of the West European communist parties and also one which has played an important role in the governing of its nation, the PCI provides an interesting case to examine the impact of a democratic environment on the theoretical evolution of a communist party. Because it is a communist party which operates in a western democratic society, the PCI's Leninist heritage has become an increasingly problematic legacy. The party's attitudes toward Leninism, in fact, have come to be seen as a test of its commitment to democratic processes and institutions as well as an indicator of its fitness to take part in the government. The PCI's leaders are not yet willing to renounce Leninism completely. However, in recent years, they have moved beyond efforts to reinterpret Lenin's teachings to the more open admission that Leninism is no longer relevant as a guide to the building of socialism in developed western countries.

This process, which can in certain respects be traced to the decision to seek power by democratic means after the second World War, has been given added impetus by events in the Soviet Union and Eastern Europe as well as by the PCI's electoral fortunes at home. In its early stages, the PCI's effort to adapt its doctrines to domestic circumstances led the party's leaders to argue that each communist party should find its own road to socialism. As articulated by Palirmo Togliatti, the Italian Road to Socialism, or <u>Via italiana al socialismo</u>, envisioned a peaceful transition to socialism in Italy, a transition which would be accomplished through the use of existing parliamentary and electoral institutions.

In the last decade, this early divergence from Leninist theory concerning the means to be used to

60

achieve socialism has been supplemented by different
views regarding the nature of socialism itself.
Particularly after the forcible end of the reform
process in Czechoslovakia in 1968, the PCI's leaders have enunciated views which differ considerably
from those we associate with Leninism concerning
the characteristics of the future socialist society,
the role of the communist party, and its relations
with other political forces. At the same time, however, the party's leaders have continued to affirm
the validity of certain Leninist tenets, including
democratic centralism as a principle of internal
organization. They have also sought to maintain
the PCI's identity as a distinctly communist party.
As part of this effort, they have highlighted the
ways in which they differ from the social democrats
and emphasized their continued desire to transform
capitalist society, albeit by democratic methods.
    Recent polemics with the Italian socialists
and the discussions occasioned by the PCI's XV Party Congress illustrate both of these tendencies.
The deletion of explicit references to Leninism
from the party's statutes should not be seen as a
weakening of the party's commitment to radical
transformation of Italian society. Rather, it has
been accompanied by attempts to provide a domestic,
rather than Leninist, basis for this commitment.
The pages to follow examine the extent to which the
PCI has diverged from Leninism and the limits of
that divergence; they then discuss the effort which
the PCI's leaders have made to find domestic roots
for the party's communist identity, with particular
attention to the newly proposed Third Way to socialism, La terza via.

COMING TO TERMS WITH LENINISM

    The PCI's attitudes toward its Leninist heri-
tage have been a frequent topic of political discussion in Italy in the post-World War II era. Often
tied to discussion of the party's links to the Soviet Union and other ruling communist parties, this
subject once again came to the forefront of political debate in Italy in the summer of 1978, largely
as the result of polemics initiated by the Italian
Socialist Party (PSI). The latest in a long series
of PSI-PCI debates over this issue, the most recent
discussions were sparked by an article published in
the weekly L'Espresso in which Bettino Craxi,
leader of the PSI, disputed the Italian communists'
claim to be elaborating a third way to socialism

61

and called on the party's leaders to clarify the party's position in regard to Leninism once and for all.[1]

The polemics, as well as the discussions which occurred prior to and during the XV Congress, centered around several major issues: first, what is and what should be the party's attitude toward its Leninist heritage in general? To what extent is Leninism still useful as a source of inspiration or as a guide to action in the Italian situation? How should the party view its application in other historical and geographic contexts? Second, which aspects of Leninist doctrine should be deleted or retained? What elements are salvageable, and which has history by-passed? Finally, what is to replace Leninism as a source of legitimacy for the party and theoretical justification for its actions? While this paper will focus on the theoretical aspects of these debates, discussion of these issues often has been connected to the party's evaluation of existing socialist countries, as well as to its alternative vision of the nature of socialist society.

In the course of these discussions, the PCI's leaders and intellectuals affiliated with the party reiterated and clarified the party's answers to these questions. With a few significant exceptions the answers given were not novel, for the process of coming to terms with Leninism as a body of thought and with the PCI's Leninist past has been occurring for some time. Nonetheless, the debates are worth examining, for they focused public attention on the issue and provoked a good deal of debate within the PCI as well. The statements made by party leaders and intellectuals during these discussions also provide the most recent and clearest statements of party views on these matters.

While the PCI's leaders maintain that they have no intention of renouncing the party's history,[2] they have adopted an increasingly differentiated and critical approach to the party's Leninist legacy. Thus, while leaders such as Berlinguer continue to note the important contribution Lenin and Leninist theory have made to the history of the workers' movement as well as to world history more generally,[3] the party's statements concerning Leninism have been informed by a more realistic and critical assessment of its value and consequences in particular historical situations. This assessment in many cases has involved the frank admission of ambiguities in Lenin's writings and, in some instances, the explicit rejection of certain aspects of Leninist theory. To a certain degree, the party's leaders have attempted to disassociate themselves from the illiberal, undemocratic elements of Leninism while retaining the party's links with the revolutionary elan and mystique which apparently still surround Lenin and his doctrines in the eyes of certain of the party's members and supporters.

This dual attitude is evident in the party's recent statements concerning the October Revolution. One of the key issues in the polemics between the PSI and PCI spokesmen, the party's evaluation of the current significance of the October Revolution has served as a touchstone to measure its divergence from Soviet doctrine and experience in regard to the proper way to establish a socialist system. Part of the broader question of the PCI's attitudes toward the value of Soviet and East European experience, this issue has been linked to the question of the party's relations with the ruling communist parties as well. In reply to socialist critiques, the PCI's leaders have reiterated earlier statements concerning the world significance of the October Revolution.[4] They have also continued to defend the Bolsheviks' choice of a violent seizure of power as the correct decision in the concrete circumstances which existed at the time in Russia.[5]

However, despite statements such as these, the party's attitudes toward the Revolution have changed substantially in recent years. While PCI leaders continue to commemorate the anniversary of the Revolution and note its importance, particularly in the party's mass circulation publications, this type of rhetoric has become less frequent. It has also been replaced to a large extent by an evaluation more in keeping with the party's often repeated commitment to establishing socialism by means of the democratic process. As Luciano Gruppi noted in a 1978 article in Critica marxista, the PCI's theoretical monthly, "if the Russian revolution is not to be relegated to the margins of the workers' movement, it is (nonetheless) clear that this (event) cannot today assume the exemplary character which communists for a long time attributed to it."[6] Similar views were expressed by party leaders in a roundtable discussion organized on the 1978 anniversary of the Revolution.[7]

While the party's attitude concerning the October Revolution reflects the judgment that Leninism was an appropriate guide to analysis and action in that specific historical and geographic context, the

63

PCI's leaders have taken very different positions in regard to its consequences in present day Soviet and Eastern European societies as well as its utility as a reference point in the Italian situation. These positions, which reflect in part the results of the critical analysis of Soviet and East European experience by party intellectuals in the past decade,[8] are evident in PCI criticism of the type of socialism which exists in current communist-led states and also in the party's analysis of the causes of the deformation of socialism in those societies. The results of these analyses are particularly interesting in the Soviet case, for party intellectuals, including Giuseppe Boffa, have gone beyond the standard party version of Soviet history to examine and probe the consequences of choices made in the early years.[9] As part of this process, PCI leaders and intellectuals have looked at the responsibility which Lenin had for the suppression of dissent within the communist party and the beginning of the system which later evolved into Stalinism. Thus while Stalin is still blamed for distorting and deforming the original Soviet system, certain analysts also admit the role which Lenin had in laying the foundations for later undemocratic developments. For the most part, these actions of Lenin's are attributed to unforeseen circumstances in early Soviet history which forced him to change his pre-revolutionary views concerning democracy and the need for political opposition.[10] These explanations have been coupled with efforts to emphasize the democratic aspects of Lenin's writings.

At the same time, PCI leaders have also discussed the existence of undemocratic passages in Lenin's writings. These discussions have been accompanied by explicit criticism of certain of Lenin's views and the open admission that Leninism has little relevance to the effort to create socialism in advanced western countries. One such area concerns Lenin's views of the value of democratic institutions. The PCI's divergence on this point pre-dates the most recent debates on Leninism, for the party's leaders have consistently affirmed their support of the existing political system and their desire to seek power by democratic means. In recent years, however, PCI spokesmen have become more explicit in affirming the party's desire not only to achieve power by democratic means, but also to maintain democratic institutions once a socialist system is established. The frequently made assertion that the PCI views democracy, including formal guarantees of democratic liberties and rights, as a universal value, one which must be maintained under socialism,[11] has been accompanied by the argument that Lenin was wrong in his evaluation of the value of democratic parliamentary institutions. To a certain extent, PCI discussions of this issue point to the changes which have occurred in Italy, as well as in certain other developed western countries, which allow the working class to work within the existing political system to transform it, as the main factor leading to the party's changed view of the importance of democratic institutions.

This argument has been restated most clearly recently by Luciano Gruppi, who identified this area as one where the PCI diverges most notably from Lenin's theories. Arguing that, contrary to Lenin's view that such institutions must be overthrown, history has shown the value of such institutions in guaranteeing the exercise of democratic liberties, Gruppi identified the new relationship between the working class and democratic institutions as the main explanation for the PCI's views concerning the importance of preserving and working through such institutions. In terms which have become common in discussing this issue, Gruppi traced the new value of democratic institutions to the important role which the working class and the PCI as its representative have had in the development of the democratic state in Italy in the post-World War II period:

> Beginning exactly from the link established by Lenin between democracy and socialism, one goes beyond Lenin, establishing a new relationship between the revolutionary struggle of the working class for socialism and those democratic institutions which are the historic contribution of the bourgeoisie. We are in a situation which is historically new, however, in respect to that in which Lenin lived. We are no longer in the historical phase in which parliamentary democracy was the conquest of bourgeois hegemony...We are in a situation in which it becomes increasingly difficult for the bourgeoisie to exercise its own hegemony in the framework of democracy; in which, beginning with the antifascist liberation struggle, the working class made itself the leading force for the struggle for democracy, as in succeeding years, it defended the republican constitution and parliamentary regime.[12]

65

But, while Gruppi's analysis implies that democratic institutions have taken on a new significance due to changes in the current Italian situation, other PCI spokesmen at times have argued that democratic institutions and guarantees are also necessary in all socialist societies, including the Soviet Union and the East European countries.[13] The negative experiences which have resulted in these societies due to the suspension of democratic rights and the stifling of political opposition are also introduced as evidence of the need to safeguard and maintain such rights and institutions.[14]

In addition to this disagreement with Leninism concerning the value of democratic institutions, the PCI has come to hold views concerning the nature of a socialist society and the role of the communist party which also diverge markedly from standard Leninist tenets. In the first area, PCI spokesmen have repeatedly stated the party's wish to avoid the violations of democratic rights and procedures which have occurred in Eastern Europe and the Soviet Union and argued that they wish to establish a socialist system which will maintain and extend current democratic practices. Part of this divergence from the type of society which has become associated with Leninism involves the role of the communist party itself. As will be discussed in more detail when we look at the PCI's own vision of socialism, the party's leaders argue that the communist party, even once socialism is established, should remain a part of the society. Having abandoned the concept of the dictatorship of the proletariat some time ago as incompatible with their image of a democratic socialist society, the PCI's leaders have emphasized the ways in which the Italian party has for some time diverged in both its organization and practice from a small, cadre-based Leninist party.[15] Still another aspect of the PCI's views of the political organization of socialism which differs from Leninism is the expectation that other parties will continue to exist.

The PCI has also altered its position in regard to Leninism in another important respect recently. In contrast to Soviet and East European practice, the party has downgraded Leninism from the preeminent intellectual and theoretical influence on the PCI to merely one of many. This action has been coupled with the elimination of the obligation of party members to adhere to Leninism and increased emphasis on the "lay" character of the PCI as a party. As part of this effort, the party's leaders have emphasized those passages of the party statutes which note that membership in the party is to be based solely on agreement with its political program. They have also taken steps to make membership in the party compatible with Catholicism by arguing that the PCI as a party does not profess atheism.[16]

This process was carried to its logical conclusion in the removal of explicit references to Leninism from the party statutes at the XV Party Congress. Justified on the basis that the formula "Marxism-Leninism" was too rigid to express the richness of the party's theoretical and ideological sources,[17] this action represented the culmination of a process which has been occurring over a period of years, rather than an abrupt break with the PCI's past. To some extent a formalization of what had already occurred in practice, this step is nonetheless significant, for it illustrates how far the PCI has departed from its former reliance on the Leninist tradition. It also is a natural outcome of the party's judgment concerning the limited value of Leninism as a guide to action or source of legitimacy in a democratic environment.

While the actions taken at the XV Party Congress thus have formalized the distance the PCI has traveled from Leninism, the party has not completely renounced all aspects of this tradition. The chief elements which the PCI seeks to retain appear to be two. First, party leaders continue to attribute some validity to Lenin's analysis of capitalism in the age of imperialism. Although party leaders at times argue for the need for new approaches to understand the nature of the current crisis which capitalism is undergoing, the teachings of Lenin in regard to world imperialism continue to be reflected in PCI analyses.[18]

The chief example of the continued influence of the PCI's Leninist heritage, however, is in the area of party organization. Despite a good deal of discussion of this issue the PCI continues to affirm the value of democratic centralism as a principle of internal party organization. One of the areas in which outsiders have been most critical of the party, it is also the issue on which the party's leaders have changed least. Certain intellectuals, such as Giulio Procacci, have argued that the entire structure of the party, including the operation of democratic centralism, is in need of rethinking,[19] while others have pointed out the potential conflicts between the PCI's vision of a

67

democratic socialist society and democratic centralism.[20]  However, these appear to be minority view-
points, for the principle was retained at the XV
Party Congress.  In polemics with the socialists and
in the pre-congress discussions, party leaders and
intellectuals defended democratic centralism on several grounds.

First, efforts have been made to distinguish
democratic centralism as it operates in the PCI from
the type of democratic centralism which prevails in
the present day Soviet and East European parties.
Noting that the principle as it was applied in Lenin's day in the Soviet Union also differed from that
which prevails today, PCI leaders have also argued
that democratic centralism works very differently in
a mass party such as the PCI than in small, clandestine parties.  This claim, often made by party leaders, is substantiated by the observations of certain
non-communist analysts.[21]  Party spokesmen also defend the principle by emphasizing the democratic
elements in the operation of democratic centralism.
Pointing out that the principle, when properly understood, is designed to allow free discussion and in-
put into decision-making before a decision is
reached, they argue that such a system is more democratic in its outcome than one which would allow organized factions, which have a tendency to thwart
the will of broad segments of a party's members.[22]

But the main ground given for retaining democratic centralism is the usefulness of the concept.
Attempting to defend democratic centralism from any
necessary links with an authoritarian, clandestine
style of politics, party leaders argue that all modern political parties have need of some type of hierarchical structure.  Given this fact, democratic
centralism is both an appropriate and necessary
principle for the PCI, it is claimed, for it allows
the party to be united enough to carry out its many
tasks in Italian society.[23]

The PCI's leaders are able to reconcile their
support for democratic centralism with their vision
of a pluralistic socialism because of the distinction noted earlier between the party and the state.
Given their argument that the party is no longer to
be seen as the prefiguration of the future socialist
state, party leaders argue that the organizing principles of the party and state do not have to coincide.  In arguments which are reminiscent of the
views on political and social organization expressed
by numerous other thinkers, some of them within the
democratic tradition,[24] PCI spokesmen claim that it

68

is entirely possible for the party and other elements of socialist society to be governed by different organizational tenets. In the course of the pre-congress discussions, Alberto Scarponi argued that democratic centralism might provide a useful tool to increase the participation of all citizens in political life,[25] but this argument is unusual. For the most part, PCI leaders and intellectuals maintain that they have no intention of extending the operation of democratic centralism beyond the limits of the communist party.

With the exception of its continued reliance on democratic centralism then, the PCI's doctrines bear little relation to Leninism as the term is generally understood. While the behavior of the party's officials and representatives has for some time conformed to the requirements of democratic political rules, it is only in the past year that party leaders have brought the party's theoretical formulations into conformity with this behavior. Given the importance which links to the Leninist tradition have played in legitimizing the party and differentiating it from other political forces in Italy, it is perhaps understandable that the PCI's leaders were reluctant to make their divergences from this tradition explicit. By doing so, they have given rise to the issue of how the party's distinctly communist identity is to be maintained.

## IN PLACE OF LENINISM: DOMESTIC ROOTS AND THE THIRD WAY

As the result of their increasingly explicit move away from Leninism, the leaders of the PCI have been faced with the need to develop a new basis for the party's claim to be a proponent of radical transformation. Arguing that their move away from Leninism does not signify a renunciation of the party's communist identity, the PCI's leaders have attempted to maintain this identity in several ways.

As the significance of Lenin's writings has been downplayed, the PCI's leaders and intellectuals affiliated with the party have attempted to fill this gap by turning to other thinkers as sources of inspiration. An effort to broaden the PCI's intellectual heritage, this process has been evident in the increased attention given to other Marxist writers. Recent commentaries on Bauer in _Rinascita_, for example, have argued that his writings and views should be seen as part of the communist as well as social-democratic tradition.[26] PCI scholars and

69

spokesmen have also shown a good deal of interest in the writings of Bukharin in recent years.[27]

Increasingly, however, the PCI's leaders have attempted to base the party's communist identity firmly on domestic, Italian roots. On the theoretical plane, this effort is evident in the increased coverage given to Italian socialists and thinkers, including Labriola and Gramsci, as sources of the party's views. In the case of Gramsci, this process is of course a delicate one, for, as PCI spokesmen admit, there are numerous Leninist elements in Gramsci's theories. The party's response to this fact has been a dual one. Party leaders have at times disassociated the PCI from certain of Gramsci's views, particularly those concerning the organization of the communist party and the characteristics of the future socialist society,[28] but the more common act has been to focus on Gramsci's stature as an original Marxist thinker and the importance which his early adaptation of Marxism to Italian conditions had for the subsequent development of the PCI. PCI spokesmen often point to this adaptation as evidence that the party never accepted Marxism or Leninism passively, but, from its inception, modified these doctrines to fit the Italian context.[29] Concepts derived from Gramsci's writings also continue to influence the PCI's phraseology and analyses. This influence is especially apparent in the party's emphasis on the importance of the cultural aspect of the effort to achieve socialism as well as in the references which party leaders continue to make to the hegemony of the working class.

The highlighting of the PCI's links to indigenous thinkers has been accompanied by a renewed emphasis on the domestic basis of the party's appeal and success. In replies to critics who pointed to the Leninist heritage of the party, PCI spokesmen have argued that the party's links to the world communist movement and the Leninist tradition have not been the main reason for its success. Rather, the argument is made, the party's stature depends on its own record of actions in the Italian context. Thus, certain of the PCI's leaders have dismissed the issue of the party's connection with Leninism as secondary, claiming that the real basis for judging the party should be its efforts and achievements on behalf of the Italian working class.[30]

A final part of the PCI's effort to find a domestic base for its claim to be a force working for significant change in Italian society, despite its renunciation of Leninism, is evident in the newly outlined concept of socialism, *La terza via*, or the Third Way. A term which first came into use during the summer of 1978, *La terza via* is said to describe a type of socialism which will differ in important ways from that which exists in the Soviet Union and Eastern Europe, but also from social democracy. Depicted as an effort to elaborate a type of socialism suited to the needs of developed western countries, the Third Way, party leaders claim, outlines a means of avoiding the undemocratic aspects of the Soviet and East European experience, while at the same time achieving significant transformation of capitalist society. As in recent discussions of Leninism, the party's leaders have emphasized their distance from *both* earlier socialist traditions and argued that they are elaborating a new, original path to socialism, one built upon the party's previous actions in Italy and particularly suited to Italian reality.

While PCI leaders continue to eschew the task of predicting the forms and characteristics of the future society, *La terza via* may be seen as the positive counterpart to the party's critiques of the Soviet and East European experiences on the one hand and social democracy on the other. Although party spokesmen and intellectuals emphasize that the Third Way should be seen not as a model, but as a "research design," or framework for further discussion,[31] it provides the clearest elaboration to date of the party's vision of socialism. Described by party leaders as an updating and extension of the *Via Italiana al socialismo* to the European plane, the Third Way is held to be a type of socialism appropriate for advanced, western countries. As elaborated in the Draft Statutes and a roundtable discussion in *Rinascita* in January 1979, *La terza via* summarizes the party's views in three main areas. First, it outlines the PCI's conception of the nature of the state and role of the communist party in socialist society. Second, it discusses the economic organization of society, including the place of private property under socialism. Finally, the term clarifies the PCI's position concerning the role of ideology in the state and for the party. In line with the renewed emphasis on the domestic roots of the PCI's appeal and identity, party leaders and intellectuals often link discussions of these issues to past and on-going developments in Italy. Thus, the Third Way is held to be a projection into the future of trends which have already been evident in the work of the PCI and which have already begun to

71

appear in Italian society.[32]

In regard to the political organization of socialist society, discussions of the Third Way reiterate earlier PCI statements concerning the value of democratic institutions and the role of the communist party under socialism. At the same time, however, the party's leaders emphasize the need to transform existing democratic institutions to allow the masses a greater role in the governing of the country. While the Draft Theses reaffirm the PCI's often-stated belief that "political democracy thus is the highest institutional form of organization of a state, also of a socialist state," they go on to note that "the reform of the social and economic structure is essential to render democratic rights completely meaningful and effective, eliminating the exploitation and the inequalities of classes, assuring to all equal possibilities of affirming their own personalities and leading to a gradual overcoming of the division between governed and governors, to the full liberation of man and society."[33]

This emphasis on the need to expand and develop new forms of democratic participation within the framework of the existing state has also been evident in other discussions of the nature of political authority under socialism. In the course of these discussions, the PCI's leaders and intellectuals have persistently reaffirmed the party's desire to work within existing institutions, but it is clear that they do not accept the present functioning, or perhaps even form, of state authority as final. As Luciano Gruppi, in one of the more interesting of these discussions notes, the PCI envisions "not only the conquest of state power by new forces, which will leave the state as it is, but a development of the democratic institutions of the state and the overcoming of all forms of centralized, bureaucratized, and authoritarian power. This entails the transformation of the whole organization of the state. The notion of the 'smashing' of the state has not been abandoned, but assumed in a different process."[34] Elaborating on this view, other PCI spokesmen have warned that the liberal state should not be seen as the only legitimate form of democracy.[35]

Two further points stand out in the context of the PCI's discussions of the political organization of socialist society. First, as is evident in the Rinascita roundtable discussion, the Third Way is premised on the belief that the state will continue

72

to be necessary under socialism. Thus, while the party's spokesmen disassociate the PCI from the Leninist view of the bourgeois state, they also differentiate their views from those of both those European socialists who argue for "autogestion" (workers' self-management), and West European social democrats who view the current functioning of the bourgeois state as acceptable.[36] Recent discussion of the nature of political authority under socialism, however, while it has served to clarify the ways in which the PCI's views differ from those of representatives of other socialist traditions, has done little to provide us with a clearer picture of the type of transformations the PCI wishes to see or the concrete institutional forms these transformations might take. In their discussions of reform of the political system, PCI spokesmen have given most attention to the way in which current governmental institutions operate. In an emphasis later criticized as one-sided in the wake of the party's losses in the June 1979 elections, PCI leaders have proposed certain changes, including the elimination of the second chamber of the parliament, the upgrading of the staff and research facilities of deputies, reform of the central administration, and the strengthening of the powers of local governments, to improve the functioning of these institutions.[37] Scattered references to such decentralized forms of mass involvement in the political process as school councils, cultural associations, and other ad-hoc citizen groups provide some idea of the type of mechanisms which the PCI feels should supplement formal government institutions,[38] but the larger issues of how such associations should be fostered, their relation to central state authorities and to the political parties have not yet been joined. Intellectuals affiliated with the party have acknowledged the unresolved difficulties which the question of the state and the organization of political authority poses for Marxists,[39] but the recent discussions have done little to solve this problem.

Similar difficulties continue to exist in regard to the role of the communist party under socialism. Discussions of the political organization of socialist society in connection with the Draft Theses and elaborations of the Third Way have given most attention to the role of the communist party. Drawing once again on earlier statements, party spokesmen made several important points concerning the place of the PCI and other political parties in socialist society. First, they have argued that the PCI is,

73

and will remain, only a "part" of socialist society; as such it will not absorb the state or substitute itself for the operation of government institutions. These statements, which emphasize the valuable organizing function which parties perform in democratic societies, have been coupled to the explicit rejection of earlier views concerning the relation between the PCI and the future society. As expressed in the Draft Theses, the PCI is not to be seen as a "prefiguration" of the State, as Gramsci envisioned, but rather as one part of that society.[40] Furthermore, the PCI itself is seen as one of several parties which express the will of the working classes. This expectation is based on a view of socialist society which differs radically from that implicit in the Leninist heritage. In contrast to the harmonious view of social relations under socialism which prevails in the Soviet Union and Eastern Europe, PCI leaders argue that different interests, ideological traditions, and values will continue to exist after class antagonisms are eliminated. Given this fact, the party's leaders foresee the continued existence of several parties to represent the interests of the working class, as well as of other parties which do not necessarily support socialism, so long as those parties abide by democratic rules.[41]

The most troublesome aspect of recent discussions of this issue centers on the concept of "hegemony." As noted earlier, certain PCI spokesmen have explicitly rejected the concept of hegemony as inappropriate in the Italian context, as well as incompatible with the party's commitment to pluralism. Nonetheless, the concept is one which has proved more difficult than most to discard, and it occurs frequently in the statements of party leaders and intellectuals concerning the role of the party and the nature of socialism. Thus, the Draft Theses make reference to the hegemony of the working class, as well as to its "central function" in the struggle for the transformation of capitalist society, due to its objective position in the process of production and its political maturity.[42] Discussions of the Third Way also have referred to the hegemony of the working class, although party spokesmen take care to note that the working class is now expected to exercise its hegemony through numerous socialist parties and currents and as part of an alliance with progressive elements in other social classes and strata.[43] For the most part, the term seems to be used in its Gramscian sense, i.e., with reference to the

eventual cultural and intellectual predominance of
the working class. Party leaders also often refer
to the "new power bloc" which will gain predominant
influence, a concept put forward by Togliatti.[44]
Although party spokesmen also emphasize the need to
acquire this influence by means of persuasion and
obtaining the consensus of other classes and groups,
the impact of the hegemony of the working class,
whether exercised by one party or several, on the
functioning of the political system has not been
discussed in any detail. Nor have the conflicts between the party's positions in regard to hegemony
and pluralism noted by certain party intellectuals
been explored in any depth.

Although discussion of the political aspects of
the Third Way provoked a certain amount of dissent
and disagreement on the part of party members,[45] it
was the second aspect of this vision of socialism,
those portions related to the economic organization
of society, which proved to be the most controver-
sial. This controversy is evident at both the
leadership and mass levels. While there has evi-
dently been a good deal of dispute over the party's
positions in this area, the documents approved at
the XV Party Congress, as well as elite discussions
of the Third Way agree on a significant point, i.e.,
they envision the continued existence of private
property in some forms under socialism. In line
with the recent actions of PCI leaders in the economic sphere,[46] the Draft Theses state the view
that "a total nationalization of the means of production is not necessary to realize the ends and
values of socialism."[47] Rather, public and private
sectors should coexist. Accordingly, and consistent
with the party's criticism of the inefficiencies of
Soviet-type economies, the PCI's leaders have endorsed a type of socialism which will combine
planned and market elements. While the party's
spokesmen maintain that they still want to liquidate
or eliminate capitalism,[48] they now argue that certain forms of private property should be retained
under socialism. PCI spokesmen continue to argue
that large, monopolistic industries must be in the
hands of the government, but view large areas of
economic activity, including agriculture, the crafts,
and medium as well as small industry as properly
left in private hands.[49]

In line with this position against total nationalization, the party's leaders have shifted emphasis
from ownership of the means of production to social
control over planning and distribution as the

75

crucial economic issue. However, aside from what appears to be a fairly general consensus among party leaders concerning the importance of social control, there is little agreement concerning the best means to achieve such control. The roundtable discussion of the Third Way organized by <u>Rinascita</u> in January 1979 revealed some interesting differences of opinion among party leaders concerning the economic organization of socialist society. Articulating what appeared to be a minority position, Trentin, leader of the powerful metalworkers' labor union, argued that the Third Way differed from the Soviet and social democratic experiences largely by virtue of the attention it gave to self-government by the workers. Noting that both previous socialist traditions had neglected this segment of Marxist theory, Trentin emphasized the need to find mechanisms to allow the workers more influence on the planning of production and other economic decisions.[50] His views on this point, however, were challenged by several other leaders, who emphasized the need for the workers' participation in economic decision-making to be coordinated with action in the political sphere. In the words of Asor Rosa, who also warned against the perils of succumbing to the "pseudomythical" appeal of workers' self-management, "I don't think that the slogan of the day will be 'self-government by the producers,'... but rather 'government by the workers' movement.'"[51] According to this view, which appears to be the predominant one, then, greater involvement of the workers in the planning process is desirable, but such involvement must be coordinated with the political sphere and, presumably, mediated through the communist party.[52]

The final aspect of the PCI's recently proposed Third Way to socialism concerns the role of ideology in the state and in the party. An area which has received increased attention in the past few years, discussion of this issue centered around two related problems. First, what values and ideal traditions should exist during the transition to socialism? On this issue, the Draft Theses and discussions of the Third Way reconfirm the PCI's commitment to pluralism in the sphere of culture and ideas as well as politics. The Draft Theses also reaffirm the party's commitment to religious liberty and note the progressive role Christianity could play in the modern era.[53]

The more interesting aspect of the Third Way in this connection, however, concerns the party's own

76

ideology. As noted earlier, the leaders of the PCI
have argued that the rules which pertain inside the
party do not necessarily have to coincide with those
of society as a whole, given the fact that the party is, and will remain, only one part of the state.
Relying on this position, they have argued that
while the state should not have an official ideology
or belief system, the PCI, as a working class party,
may continue to draw its inspiration from particular
ideal sources. The elimination of references to
"Marxism-Leninism" from the party's statutes has
moved the PCI closer to its claims to be a "lay,"
or non-ideological, party. Nonetheless, despite
the effort to make membership in the party dependent
solely on agreement with the party's political program, as the Draft Theses note, the PCI continues
to base its analyses and activities in the tradition of scientific socialism. To the extent that it
does so, recent changes do not at all imply the party's rejection of the Marxist aspect of its heritage. At the same time, discussions of this issue
have stressed the non-dogmatic nature of the PCI's
interpretation of Marxism. PCI leaders have also
stressed the plurality of the sources which have influenced the party, with particular emphasis on indigenous Italian theorists. In this area, then, the
Third Way envisions a communist party which, though
committed to achieving socialism, draws on a variety
of cultural and moral traditions in addition to
Marxism.[54]

Part of the effort to base the party's communist
identity more firmly on domestic roots, this aspect
of the Third Way also occasioned some dissent. Despite the reaffirmation by PCI leaders that the
party remains within the Marxist segment of the socialist tradition, certain party members argued that
the changes in the area of ideology would weaken the
party's identity or its will to fight for change.[55]


SUMMARY AND CONCLUSIONS

In recent months, the leaders of the Italian
communist party have taken important steps in coming
to terms with the conflicts which their Leninist
heritage has posed in a democratic environment. One
of the more important parts of this process is the
admission that Leninism is no longer useful as a
guide to action or source of legitimacy in the Italian situation. To a large extent a formalization of
existing practice, the removal of references to

77

Leninism from the party's statutes is nonetheless significant, for it symbolizes the extent to which the PCI has departed from tenets and practices we generally associate with communist parties. As recent polemics with the Italian socialists and the discussions surrounding the XV Party Congress illustrate, however, this process should not be seen as a deradicalization of the party. While it is true that the PCI has adapted in many ways to the conditions of electoral competition in a democratic sosiety, this adaptation does not signify acceptance of all aspects of the status quo. Rather, the party's leaders continue to emphasize the PCI's commitment to working for fundamental change in Italy.

With the renunciation of the party's Leninist heritage, the PCI's leaders have been faced with the need to provide an alternate basis for the PCI's continued claim to be a communist party. This issue, which centers around the party's desire to portray itself as a political force whose aim is not simply to win a share of power in the existing system but to change that system, has generated a good deal of controversy within the PCI and in other political circles in Italy. The party's leaders have attempted to answer the question of how a party can be communist, though not Leninist, by expanding the PCI's theoretical sources and emphasizing the party's roots in the domestic Italian situation and history. This effort, which reflects a judgment that the party can base its legitimacy far more on its own actions and programs than on its ties with the international workers movement, has also been evident in more explicit attempts to fill in the outlines of the PCI's own vision of socialism. However,these attempts, which gave rise to a new PCI slogan, the Third Way to socialism, have been directed not only at differentiating the party's views from those of current communist regimes. Rather, the party's spokesmen have noted the deficiencies of social democratic as well as Leninist experiences and emphasized the ways in which the PCI's views differ from both of these traditions.

To what extent have these efforts to create a new basis for the party's identity been successful? The PCI's efforts in this respect have been challenged from several perspectives. The Italian socialists, as well as certain other segments of the political spectrum in Italy, continue to argue that "the Third Way does not exist," as Norberto Bobbio claimed in the autumn of 1978.[56] Pointing to the

PCI's stated commitment to continue to work for fundamental change as well as to its refusal to renounce all aspects of the Leninist tradition and sever its ties with the Soviet Union and other socialist states, these observers argue that the PCI must make a more fundamental choice between the methods and goals of social democracy and those of the Leninist tradition.

But, the continued dissatisfaction on the part of social democratic observers appears to be of less concern to the PCI's leaders than the reaction within certain segments of the party and the PCI's electoral supporters. The decision of the party's leaders to couple their move away from Leninism with an explicit effort to differentiate themselves from the social democratic tradition reflects a sensitivity to the problems which the PCI's recent behavior and theoretical changes have posed for the party's image, particularly among certain of the party's militants. These problems have become particularly acute in recent months, for, ironically enough, the PCI formalized its move away form the Leninist heritage soon after it left the multi-party coalition it had joined in the wake of the assassination of Aldo Moro.

The decision to leave the coalition, which has been interpreted by many observers as an effort to stem dissatisfaction resulting from the PCI's inability to effect change in return for its participation, coincided with a renewed emphasis on the party's commitment to work for transformation as well as its role as a party of "struggle."[57] The loss which the party suffered in the June 1979 elections appears to be another indication of voter dissatisfaction at the conciliatory positions taken by the PCI while part of the coalition. If, as seems plausible, it also reflects a popular view of the PCI as too well integrated into the existing system and too little interested in change, it provides a clear indication of the depth of the problem which the party's leaders face and will continue to face in the future in their efforts to fashion a new, indigenous, basis for their communist identity.


NOTES

1. Bettino Craxi, "Il Vangelo socialista," L'Espresso, August 27, 1978.
2. Enrico Berlinguer, "L'identita del PCI," L'unità, August 2, 1978, p. 2. Alessandro Natta,

"I communisti per quel che sono," <u>Rinascita</u>, no. 37, September 22, 1978, pp. 9-11.

3. Berlinguer, op. cit., p. 2.

4. See, for example, Adalberto Minucci, "In realta ci chiedono di scomunicare la storia," <u>L'unità</u>, July 30, 1978, p. 1, and Enrico Berlinguer's speech at the XV Congress in <u>L'unità</u>, March 31, 1979, pp. 9-10.

5. Berlinguer, "L'identita del PCI," p. 2; Luciano Gruppi, "Lenin, il leninismo e il Pci," <u>Critica marxista</u>, 1978, no. 5, pp. 12-13.

6. Gruppi, op. cit., p. 9.

7. Biagio Di Giovanni, "Teoria marxista e stato," <u>Critica marxista</u>, 1978, no. 3, pp. 3-18.

8. Intellectuals affiliated with the party have conducted a number of detailed studies of various aspects of the politics, economies, and societies of the Soviet Union and Eastern Europe in the past few years. The Center for the Study of the Socialist Countires, part of the Gramsci Institute, has also organized a number of conferences to present this research. Recent conferences have examined developments in Hungary, Poland, Czechoslovakia during the reform period, and workers' self-management in Yugoslavia.

9. See Boffa's <u>Storia dell'Unione Sovietica</u> (Rome: Mondadori, 1976).

10. See for example, Berlinguer, "L'identita del PCI," p. 2; Gruppi, op. Cit., pp. 10, 12.

11. This statement, which was given great prominence during the 1976 election campaigns, is still frequently reiterated by party spokesmen. See for example, Berlinguer, "L'identita del PCI," p. 11, and Gruppi, op. cit., p. 11.

12. Gruppi, op. cit., p. 16.

13. Berlinguer, "L'identita del PCI," p. 11.

14. Gruppi, op. cit., pp. 16-17.

15. Ibid., pp. 24-25.

16. "Progetto di tesi per il XV Congresso nazionale del PCI," p. 3.

17. Ibid; see also Berlinguer, "L'identita del PCI," p. 2, and Luigi Lombardo Radice, "La practica del confronto e quella del divieto," <u>L'unità</u>, February 16, 1979, p. 3.

18. See for example, Berlinguer, "L'identita del PCI," <u>L'unità</u>, March 31, 1979, p. 4.

19. Guilio Procacci, "Appunti sugli statuti del Pci dopo la Liberazione," <u>Critica marxista</u>, 1978, no. 6, pp. 69-77. Procacci also challenged the prevailing depiction of the PCI's VIII Party Congress

as the beginning of the party's decisive adaptation
to democratic conditions and argued that the party
statutes adopted at the VIII Congress actually were
a step backward in several areas, including the
interpretation they gave to democratic centralism.

20. Alessandro Natta, in his contribution to the
roundtable discussion of democratic centralism published in _Rinascita_, "Il dibattito sul centralismo
democratico," no. 31, August 10, 1979, pp. 7-10,
raised this possibility. Natta noted that the issue
of intraparty democracy is a problem not only for the
PCI, but for all political parties (p. 7).

21. See for example, Gianfranco Pasquino,
"Organizational Models of Southern European Communist
Parties: A Preliminary Approach," paper presented at
the Woodrow Wilson International Center for Scholars
Colloquium, Washington, D.C., June 14, 1979.

22. Enrico Berlinguer, "Due ore di dialogo sulle
Tesi fra Berlinguer e i gionalisti," _L'unità_, December 21, 1978, p. 4.

23. See for example, Salvatore Corallo, "Par-
liamo di come si discute in tutti i partiti,"
_Rinascita_, no. 40, October 13, 1978, pp. 10-11, and
Natta, "I communisti per quel che sono," p. 11.

24. See for example, the views of Robert A.
Dahl, _After the Revolution_ (New Haven: Yale University Press, 1970), especially pp. 77-103.

25. Alberto Scarponi, "Pci, centralismo democratico e sviluppo della democrazia," _Critica marx-
ista_, 1978, no. 5, pp. 169-70.

26. See for example, Luigi Lombardo Radice, "A
chi appertiene Otto Bauer?" _L'unità_, November 17,
1978, p. 3, and Giacomo Marramao, "Bauer, Gramsci,
'terza via,'" _Rinascita_, no. 35, November 17, 1978,
pp. 6-7.

27. This renewed interest in Bukharin's theories
and writings has been accompanied by PCI efforts to
have Bukharin rehabilitated in the Soviet Union.
See Guiliano Procacci, "Perche riabilitare Bukharin:
i conti con tutti il nostro passato," _Rinascita_, no.
26, June 30, 1979, pp. 23-24.

28. See for example, Natta, "I communisti per
quel che sono," p. 9. Luciano Gruppi, in "Lenin, il
leninismo, el il Pci," observed that "It seems to me
beyond discussion that the concept of hegemony does
not fit either in Lenin or in Gramsci with that of
pluralism." Gruppi goes on to note, however, that
the concept in its Gramscian sense signifies "political and cultural leadership, gained by consensus"
(pp. 21-22).

29. See Nicola Badoloni, "Il leninismo, la democrazia, il communismo italiano," Rinascita, no. 35, September 8, 1978, pp. 1-2.

30. Berlinguer, "L'identita del Pci," p. 2; Adalberto Minucci, "Classe operaia e societa," Rinascita, no. 38, September 29, 1978, pp. 1-2 and "Ma e possibile una soluzione moderata della crisi?" Rinascita, no. 36, September 15, 1978, pp. 3-4.

31. "La terza via al socialismo," Rinascita, no. 1, January 15, 1979, p. 7.

32. Ibid., p. 8.

33. Projetto tesi, p. 2.

34. Gruppi, op. cit., p. 18; Gruppi advanced similar arguments in "A proposito di democrazia e socialismo," Critica marxista, vol. 14, no. 2 (March-April 1976), pp. 3-20.

35. See for example, Antonio De Meo, "I nodi della sinistra in un dibattito sull 'Avanti!'" Critica marxista, 1978, no. 5, pp. 174-78.

36. "La terza via al socialismo," pp. 7-12.

37. See Luigi Berlinguer, "I bisogni nuovi della democrazia," Rinascita, no. 14, April 6, 1979, pp. 8-9 for discussions of these reforms. See the reports of the July 1979 Central Committee meeting in "Il Dibattito sulla relazione di Berlinguer," L'unita, July 6, 1979, pp. 8-10 for later criticism of this focus on reform of existing state institutions.

38. Gruppi, "A proposito di democrazia e socialismo," pp. 4-5, and Adalberto Minucci, "Discutendo con Pietro Ingrao su 'Crisi e terza via,'" Rianscita, January 26, 1979, pp. 7-9. For a more detailed examination of PCI efforts to foster decentralized forms of participation see Raymond M. Seidelman, "Reforms of the State and Communist Power," paper presented at the annual meeting of the American Political Science Association, Washington, D.C., 1979.

39. See for example, Claudia Mancina, "Il dibattito sullo Stato, Marxismi a confronto," Critica marxista, 1978, no. 5, pp. 63-77, and Leonardo Paggi, "Le forme del potere," Rinascita, no. 31, August 10, 1979, pp. 23-24.

40. Projetto tesi, p. 2.

41. Ibid., and "La terza via al socialismo," p. 10.

42. Projetto tesi, p. 2.

43. "La terza via al socialismo," pp. 8-10.

44. See for example, Gruppi, "Lenin, il leninsimo, e il Pci," p. 3 and "A proposito di democrazia e socialismo," pp. 14-15.

45. See for example, the negative judgements expressed by Lorenzo Foco and Guido Mazzoni in "La tribuna congressuale," L'unità, March 16, 1979, p. 8, and Giancarlo Bertolio, in "La tribuna congressuale," L'unità, January 19, 1979, p. 6.

46. PCI leaders have taken the unusual position in recent years of arguing for a return of certain enterprises currently owned by the state to private hands. For an examination of other aspects of the party's recent economic views, see Michael J. Sodaro, "The Italian Communists and the Politics of Austerity," unpublished manuscript.

47. Projetto tesi, p. 3.

48. See for example, Enrico Berlinguer, "L'identita del Pci," p. 11.

49. This position, which appears to be widely accepted by the party'se leaders, apparently has not been accepted as readily by certain members. As expressed in letters to L'unità published as part of the pre-congress debate, this dissent centers around the view that the party should continue to regard the elimination of private property as an eventual goal. See Valerio Caramassi, "Mutano i modi, non i fini della transizione," L'unità, February 9, 1979, p. 8, and Vittorio Aghermo, in "La tribuna congressuale," L'unità, March 16, 1979, p. 8.

50. "La terza via al socialismo," p. 10.

51. Ibid.

52. Party leaders have displayed a good deal of interest in the Yugoslav experience with workers' self-management, perhaps because the Yugoslav system combines political and economic mechanisms. See Adriano Geurra, "Studiare l'autogestione jugoslava," Rinascita, no. 13, March 30, 1979, pp. 24-25.

53. Projetto tesi, p. 3.

54. Ibid.; see also Berlinguer, "L'identita del Pci," pp. 2, 11.

55. See for example. Luigi Boccardi, "Quale socialismo e con quali forze politiche," L'unità, February 6, 1979, p. 8, and Lando Bortolotti's contribution in "La tribuna congressuale," L'unità, February 16, 1979, p. 8.

56. Norberto Bobbio, "La terza via non esista," La stampa, September 1, 1978.

57. Criticism of the party's previous strategy and renewed emphasis on the party's commitment to change prevaded the discussion of the election results at the July 1979 meeting of the PCI's central committee. See "Il dibattito sulla relazione di Berlinguer," L'unità, July 7, 1979, pp. 8 and 9 for reports of these discussions.

# 5
# Ideology and Organization in the Spanish Communist Party

*Eusebio M. Muhal-León*

The Partido Comunista de España (PCE) has for some years now been in the forefront of efforts to articulate a convincingly democratic and consensual model of socialism. That effort has led the Spanish Communists to drop all pretense of being a radical, anti-system force, committed to the violent overthrow of the existing political and social system and, instead, to become an assiduous advocate of what Santiago Carrillo has appropriately enough called "revolutionary reformism."[1]

Our concern in this chapter will be to explore those changes in the organizational and ideological dimensions of Spanish Communism. These flowed from the reevaluation of PCI policies begun by Santiago Carrillo and others in the party leadership after 1956, and they obeyed in this sense a profound domestic imperative. But there were other circumstances which affected the transformations in ideology and organization as well. Although we shall not focus explicitly on them in the course of this chapter, they help to orient our discussion and as such might be conveniently mentioned here. The first point would be to insist on the contextual importance of the fissiparous trends which manifested themselves in

---

*Parts of this chapter were presented at a March 1978 conference sponsored by the Istituto Affari Internazionali in Rome. These have been published in Lo Spettatore Internazionali and in Heinz Timmermann (ed.) The Communist Parties of Southern Europe (Nomos-Verlag). It is with their kind permission that these appear here.

the international Communist movement after the death
of Stalin in March 1953. The crisis of confidence
and leadership in the Soviet Union encouraged claims
for specific national roads to socialism and for
political and ideological independence from Moscow.
In the case of Western European parties like the
PCE or the PCI--and this brings us to our second
point--the movement away from Soviet tutelage and
toward the assumption of democratic values had as
its driving force failure, the failure of Leninism
to provide a suitable model for the successful seizure of power on the Continent. Finally, we might
insist, the growing awareness as to the bankruptcy
of Leninism should not be viewed in an ahistorical
light. Most, if not all, the issues raised and the
doctrinal/organizational innovations proposed by the
PCE and likeminded parties are not original. That
they are raised again is tribute to the fact that
after a long and sterile lapse those parties are re-
turning to the mainstream of Western European Marxist thought.

I

Already during the Spanish Civil War, the PCE
had earned a reputation as a prominent advocate of
moderation and restraint and its Popular Front experience enshrined it as the international Communist
movement's premier exponent of broad front tactics.
The Communist policy of first winning the war and
only then moving to deepen the social revolution
brought the PCE harsh criticism from left-wing Socialists and Anarchists who accused the party of
betraying the chances for a Spanish Revolution to
the imperatives of Soviet foreign policy. The
charge was not without foundation insofar as the PCE
was only too willing during the war years and after
to do Moscow's bidding. Such considerations aside,
however, what is important to remember is that the
Civil War experience was decisive in setting the political style of Spanish Communism.
That style, which emphasized broad, multi-class
alliances and a gradualist strategy of social change,
was instrumental in attracting several hundred thou-
sand Spaniards, most of whom did not belong to the
working class, to the Communist banner in the years
1936-39. Indeed, membership figures available for
1937 indicate that the PCE had become an overwhelm-
ingly middle-class organization: of the 300,000
members the party claimed that year, only 35 percent
came from the industrial working class, and even

85

that figure inflated the number of people of working class origin since it included an unspecified number of artisans and small shopkeepers.[2] This is not the place to undertake an examination of the reasons for this apparent embourgeoisement of the PCE. Most explanations suggest that the moderate line imposed on the Spanish party by Moscow made it impossible for the PCE to compete effectively with the Anarchist CNT and the Socialist UGT in the labor movement. What is important in our context is the fact that over the course of the next four decades and despite the vicissitudes of clandestinity the Spanish Communists continued to act as if their political space were still preempted on the Left.

That orientation deepened perceptibly in the mid-1950's after Santiago Carrillo assumed a dominant position within the PCE. Under his stewardship, the Spanish party promulgated its now famous call for National Reconciliation among Spaniards[3] and, in subsequent years, the PCE spared little effort in its drive to bridge the chasm which separated it from the Spanish middle classes. Symptomatic of these efforts was the posture the Spanish party adopted in 1958 with regard to the overthrow of the Franco regime. Its downfall, the Communists argued, would not result from an armed assault on the citadels of power by the opposition but would come via a largely peaceful huelga nacional. For a time, the PCE continued to insist that after Franco's overthrow his successors would have to implement profound structural reforms which would put Spain on the road to socialism; but, by the 1970's, it had abandoned that notion as well. In a well-publicized interview Carrillo gave in May 1975, he declared: "We do not champion social revolution. We do not try to impose socialism. We only want political freedoms to be restored!"[4] Even the Communist insistence that there had to be a clearcut ruptura between the Francoist past and the democratic future had lost any real meaning by late 1976 and if, in the face of the success of Adolfo Suárez' reforma política, the Spanish party held to the notion until then, the principal reason was to increase its bargaining leverage.

The broad-based approach adopted by the Spanish Communists was evident in their decision to replace the traditional Leninist notion of the worker/peasant bloc as the motor force of the revolutionary process with the more elastic idea of the alianza de las fuerzas del trabajo y de la cultura (AFTC).[5] To adhere to the Leninist formula was to insist that the alliance between the working class and non-monopolist sectors of the middle classes was inherently unstable and that competition between them had to be eventually (and, experience dictated, rather summarily) resolved. Clearly, holding out such a prospect was hardly an incentive for representatives of the middle and petty bourgeoisie to enter into alliance with the Communists. As Marxist-Leninists, the Spanish Communists could never renounce the inevitability of the destruction of all forms of private property but, by adopting the notion of the AFTC, they implied that the process would be a rather painless one. The core of the new PCE interpretation revolved around the implications of the scientific-technical revolution. That revolution, by erasing the distinction between manual and intellectual labor, produced a situation where "the forces objectively interested in joining the working class as permanent allies on the road to socialism constituted the overwhelming majority of the population." Because those interested in socialist transformations were so numerous, the Left would have the leisure of making change gradual and the reduction in the number and influence of the middle classes would be more a consequence of atrophy than anything else.

One consequence of adopting a gradualist strategy of social change was the abandonment on the Spanish Communist part of the classical Leninist thesis that monopoly capitalism, as the highest stage of capitalist development, could only be followed in rather direct fashion by socialism. The PCE, like most of its European co-religionists, came up with the notion of an anti-monopolist democracia política y social as a stage lasting for several decades and serving as a relatively painless "transition to the transition." During this phase, social and private forms of property would coexist in relative harmony, the latter "play(ing) the same complementary role it has in the present system." 6 Government would control profits through tax measures but would insure these were sufficient to stimulate private initiative. The principal economic measures to be adopted during this phase (the nationalization of banking, credit facilities and large industrial concerns, a reform of the fiscal system and the state planning apparatus, a reorientation of enterprises already under state control, a revision of the social security system and the initiation of an agrarian reform) would be directed at the large, 'monopolistic and latifundist' concerns. Their owners would be paid compensation: the PCE

87

Program Manifesto, although silent on the critically important question of what specific formula would be used in determining how much would be owed, justified such a payment on the grounds that "the working class finds it's cheaper, when possible, to pay a compensation, however unjust it may be from the point of view of equality, to a group of property owners who would otherwise be difficult to replace."[7] In agriculture as in industry, the expropriation of property belonging to multi-national concerns would only be undertaken if these could be replaced or managed by national technology. With the capture of the commanding heights of the economy, a ruling coalition of the Left could direct Spanish society toward further socialization without risking an undue (or premature, it should be added) polarization of political life. Too precipitate a pace of social transformation, the Allende experience in Chile taught the Spanish Communists, would lead to the flight of capital and trained personnel and would only erode popular support for the new government.

The failure of those predictions the Communists made in the late 1950's and early 1960's about the imminent overthrow of the regime contributed to the proliferation of ultra-Left groups in the country. Most of them objected to the politics of National Reconciliation--they saw in its emphasis on peaceful change a capitulation to the Spanish bourgeoisie-- and reaffirmed their belief not only in the idea that the fall of Franco was near but that the socialist revolution had become the order of the day. Evoking the authority of Mao Tse-tung and Fidel Castro, they criticized the huelga nacional as 'pacifist' and as an abandonment of traditional Leninist doctrine. They may have been correct in this latter assessment, but their calls for armed insurrection were even more out of touch with reality than official party policy.

A much more serious ideological--but not organizational--challenge developed for Carrillo within the party when two members of the Executive Committee, Fernando Claudín and Jorge Semprún, criticized the faulty analysis which lay behind PCE predictions.[8] Both men had played important roles in party affairs after 1956 (Claudín was thought by many to be second in influence only to Carrillo and Semprún had been in charge of party organization in Madrid during the tumultuous years of 1957-62) and had supported the renovation Carrillo had initiated. They parted company with the PCE Secretary General and others in the leadership in the early 1960's

88

over what they perceived as the blind official insistence that the regime was more isolated with each passing day and would soon fall. The more theoretically inclined of the two, Claudín argued that an incorrect analysis of the socio-economic basis of the regime lay behind the 'voluntarist' and 'subjectivist' view of the party leadership. Carrillo and the others had misjudged the profundity of the change which Spanish society and economy had experienced since the end of the Civil War. This prevented them from recognizing that political power in Spain could shift from a conservative faction to a more liberal one, with no change in the fundamental structure of the state monopoly capitalist system and no social revolution. Such a liberalization could lead, Claudín argued, to the establishment of a Western European style parliamentary democracy and even the legalization of the Communist party, albeit under a temporary cover like that of the EDA in Greece a decade and a half before. At the same time, he insisted, because the economic system of Spain had developed to the highest stage of capitalism (namely, the state monopoly one), it was inevitable that any revolution have a socialist character.

By arguing in this fashion, Claudín sought to bridge the chasm which had been developing (and continued with even greater force) between revolutionary rhetoric and reformist practice, the latter clearly manifested in the inability to force a change in the regime. He and Semprún believed (and history appears to have vindicated them on this score as on several others) that the unwillingness of Carrillo and others in the leadership to realize or accept that a revolutionary situation did not and would not for some time exist in Spain would only exacerbate tensions within the party and between the party and various splinter groups which had been spawned in reaction to the failure of the policies and predictions of the PCE.

Criticized by the majority in the Executive Committee for their 'rightist' deviations, Claudín and Semprún were relieved of their duties at a March 1964 meeting of the Executive Committee and were formally expelled a year later. Unlike so many other Communist dissidents neither man took the subsequent step of organizing a rival group and thus the immediate organizational consequences of the affair were limited. Looked at from a longer-range perspective, however, the PCE suffered from the loss of some of its best and most incisive thinkers.

Carrillo subsequently incorporated many (although certainly not all) of their ideas, but their belated perception of the possibility and viability of a reformist solution to the Franco problem would damage the party and its credibility.

## II

We have emphasized how the inability of the Anarchists and Socialists to adapt effectively to changes in Spanish social structure and syndical legislation permitted the Communists to develop an important presence among the working class. Even while emphasizing the decisive importance of that sector to the realization of Spanish Communist objectives, however, PCE leaders tried always to avoid (not always successfully) that sectarian, ouvriériste orientation which, it has so often been noted, has been the defining characteristic of its Portuguese neighbor. The Spanish Communist party may have preferred to rely on its working class base for support during the most difficult moments of the anti-Franco struggle, but it invariably sought to expand its audience beyond the confines of the proletariat and to court the middle classes.

With socialism not a near-term possibility for Spanish society, the party adopted as its own the Gramscian notion that revolutionary change in advanced industrial societies required that the forces of the Left not only destroy or radically transform those instruments of coercion and direct domination which make up the State but also (and this is a prior condition) break the ascendance or hegemony of 'bourgeois' ideology in society. The PCE saw the road to socialism in Spain as a long one. Only after the working class and its allies (joined in the alianza de las fuerzas del trabajo y de la cultura) had first broken the spiritual and cultural hegemony of the 'ruling' class could they go about assuming plenary powers and definitively establishing socialist relations of production.[9]

In line with this sort of thinking, the Spanish Communists saw the vulnerability of the present-day capitalist State as exploitable primarily by a strategy which emphasized reform over revolution. As Marxists, they continued to view the State as the instrument for the exercise of organized violence by one class over another and regarded its takeover as the core problem of the political process. Their stratagem for dealing with this problem differed from the traditional Leninist one, however. The

Bolshevik leader had devised a rather simple and direct approach on this point, arguing that the bourgeois State had to be seized, violently destroyed, and a dictatorship of the proletariat established as a condition for the construction of socialism to begin. The Spanish Communists, by contrast, stressed the complexity of the relation of State to society in the latter part of the twentieth century and insisted it was no longer simply a matter of "destroying the State, but rather of eliminating those sectors in the (State) machine which are the expression, the instrument of monopolistic rule (the political police, top administrators, reactionary sectors in the army, finance and so on) and neutralizing and even winning over one part of the State machine by a democratic and even socialist transformation."[10]

PCE spokesmen rationalized their party's shift on the State and on the means to be employed in its transformation by pointing to changes in the role of the Spanish State and in the structure of Spanish society. The modern State, the argument went, could no longer give the impression of impartiality to other sectors of the middle class and had become instead the "exclusive instrument" of monopoly capital. This change in the nature of the State or, more precisely, in how non-monopoly sectors of the bourgeoisie viewed it was symptomatic of the deep gulf separating the interests of the monopolies from those of the rest of society. Because the monopolies represented such a small proportion of the national electorate, they could easily be defeated by an alliance between disgruntled sectors of the middle classes on the one hand and the fuerzas del trabajo y de la cultura on the other.[11] Under these circumstances, the State was not as impregnable as it may have at first glance appeared.

The second proposition advanced by the PCE with respect to the State referred to the transformation undergone by Spanish society over the course of the last four decades (but particularly since the end of autarchy) and the subsequent adoption of the Stabilization Plan in 1959. Those changes--similar and parallel developments had taken place in other Western European countries much earlier but particularly after World War II--had had a rather significant impact on the State and caused it to assume many social welfare functions. Individuals like Rudolf Hilferding of the Austro-Marxist school had already begun to describe and analyze this evolution in the second decade of this century, but Communist ideologues refused for quite some time to accept

91

such notions. When they did (and the Italian Communists were probably the first to admit it), this was primarily because they had to find some way of justifying the failure to accomplish the revolution and of maintaining the élan of their militants as to the eventual success of socialism. The Spanish Communists also shifted their views on that score and argued beginning in the 1960's that the assumption on the part of the State of social responsibilities like social security, education and the like made it impossible to define the State simply as the instrument for 'bourgeois' domination of the proletariat.[12] The growth of state intervention in the economy and the consequent expansion of the public sector also meant, in the Spanish Communist estimation, that the objective conditions for socialism were becoming ever more ripe. The change in the character and function of the State had also led to an expansion in the number of government functionaries and, since most of these employees supposedly came from the lower social classes, the PCE argued that a certain proceso de democratización had begun and would continue in the "mass of the State machine."[13]

Santiago Carrillo's "Eurocomunismo" y Estado, published in early 1977 prior to the legalization of the party, contains the most explicit and complete statement the Spanish Communists have yet made on their strategy with respect to the State and bourgeois society. There, Carrillo urged the PCE and other forces on the Left to concentrate their efforts on undermining those ideological and coercive apparatuses (the former include the Church, the educational system, the judiciary and mass media; the latter, the armed forces and other organs of 'direct' repression) which have traditionally functioned as sustaining elements of the existing order. Those apparatuses can, in his words, be "transformed and used, if not totally, then in part against the power of the state monopoly capitalist system."

Although on occasion PCE spokesmen appeared ready to embrace the notions about the evolutionary transition to socialism earlier advanced by such revisionist betes noires as Karl Kautsky and Eduard Bernstein—thus, Carrillo at one point insisted that the advance towards socialism "would not be the consequence of coercive measures but rather of the development of productive forces"[15]—for the most part they warned that it would be illusory to suppose such a transformation would come about through una

92

_acción puramente cultural e ideológica_. Even during the most peaceful of processes, there would still be a necessity for a moment of _ruptura_ at which time qualitative changes in the political and economic structures would result from coincident mass pressure outside the government and transformation of the _aparato del estado_ from within. At this point, the working class and its allies would assume complete hegemony within society but, because popular support would be so overwhelming, they need not exercise that hegemony through the classical dictatorship of the proletariat. More moderate, sophisticated and less drastic measures would suffice and could be perfectly compatible with the continuation of a parliamentary democracy. Such a view, it should be stressed, became official PCE doctrine only in the mid-1970's and at the 8th PCE Congress in August 1972 party leaders held to the idea that a dictatorship of the proletariat had not become anachronistic, even while insisting that it was the "broadest and most complete democracy."[16] Despite ambiguities which we shall take up shortly, the substance of Spanish Communist evolution on this score went beyond that of the French and Portuguese parties who also dropped the phrase.

The change in the Spanish Communist perception of the State and of the strategy for bringing about societal change also led to a revision of the role trade unions might play in that process. A revolutionary strategy premised on reforms, the PCE concluded, meant that the labor movement could no longer depend on narrow trade union organizations whose structures depended exclusively on membership.[17] Communists active in the labor movement had to create a _sindicato de nuevo tipo_ which would rely for legitimacy on factory councils and as a result would break down the barrier between _afiliado_ and _no afiliado_. It would be better able than traditional trade unions (whose orientation and structures were primarily _defensive_) to help break down capitalist control of the organization of production and to relate problems at the factor level to those which affected _la condición obrera_ in its entirety. Actively cooperating with the political parties of the Left but avowedly supra-partisan, the _sindicato de nuevo tipo—Comisiones Obreras_ in the Spanish context—could help create elements of socialism at the enterprise level.

As might be expected, the programmatic redefinitions which Santiago Carrillo and others in the PCE leadership supported came in for sharp criticism from

93

others within the party and outside it. Some of these harbored either pro-Soviet or pro-Chinese sympathies and railed against the abandonment of pristine Leninist principles. Enrique Líster, for example, accused Carrillo of being nothing more than an eurooportunista. Other, more significant criticisms came from the group coalescing around Manuel Sacristán and the journal Materiales and former PCE Executive Committee member Fernando Claudín.[18] Although by no means in total agreement with each other, Claudin and Sacristan criticized what they saw as the theoretical eclecticism and vacuousness into which the PCE was falling and the pollyannish view of the State propounded by Communist leaders. Sacristan and his supporters decried the idea that the socialization of the aparato del estado would come about through the entry of people from lower classes into the State. This, they claimed, overestimated the possible efficacy of efforts at penetration of the State apparatuses: not only had most parts of the State been impregnated by a lógica de la rentabilidad (which made them unusable for socialist purposes) but most of the critical decision-making centers had been shifted from domestic to multi-national points.[19] Spanish Communist advocacy of a relatively long transition period characterized by relative social peace (the democracia política y social) also came under fire as unrealistic. Arguing that as shrewd a politician as Carrillo could not believe in this scenario and held to it only for propagandistic reasons, Claudín insisted that with its strong anti-capitalist thrust the democracia could not be held for long at the merely anti-monopolist level.[20] Another point of criticism related to the supposed 'proletarization' of the fuerzas de la cultura, a notion upon which so many of the positions adopted by the PCE hinged. This was, in the view of the critics, at best a tendential process and qualitative modifications were necessary in technology, science, and the organization of the work before these could serve the socialist society.[21]

III

The shift away from the traditional Leninist emphasis on the quick and violent seizure of political power led the PCE to argue in favor of a slow and measured advance in the direction of socialism so as to make possible the long-awaited consummation of the marriage between political and economic democracy. For many years, the PCE shared the assessment

Lenin had made of 'bourgeois' liberties--freedom of assembly, he declared to the first Comintern Congress in 1919, was "an empty phrase in the most democratic of bourgeois republics"[22]--and its decision to defend the democratic model of socialism has to be considered an important milestone in the evolution of the Spanish party. No longer do the Spanish Communists see political and civil rights as something simply to be manipulated and used by those forces interested in forcing the overthrow of the existing order. Thus, the Political Resolution of the 8th PCE Congress described their vision of socialist society as one in which there would be respect for fundamental political liberties, freedom of information and criticism, freedom of artistic and intellectual creation, the renunciation of any attempt to impose an official state philosophy, and political pluralism into the indefinite future.[23] More recently, Santiago Carrillo has called on Communists to have "a more fundamental appreciation of democracy"[24] and Manuel Azcárate, in a remarkable essay in the journal Argumentos, has declared that "liberty was a metapolitical necessity of social progress." (Emphasis added)[25]

Promises of fidelity to fundamental liberties have appeared in the communiques signed by the PCE with the French and Italian Communists in 1975 and 1977 and in the proyecto de constitución presented to the Spanish people prior to the June 1977 election.[26] In the latter respect, it should also be noted that the Communists proposed the inclusion in the new Constitution of an estatuto de libertades guaranteeing personal liberties, freedom of assembly, the inviolability of the home and correspondence, freedom of religion and expression and the right to travel freely within and outside Spain. These principles would not be simply declarative: the State would be under a legal obligation actively to defend them. Indicating that his party now shares such fundamental liberal notions as the principle of alternation of power and understands the importance of respecting the political and social rights of minorities, Carrillo has on more than one occasion promised that it would always abide by the electoral verdict.

The vision of a society where socialism and democracy are complementary notions is, as the Spanish Communists are well aware, extremely attractive, particularly as it contrasts so vividly with the realities of Soviet and Eastern European practice. In advocating such a model, the PCE has gone quite a distance away from Leninism's singular and, one might say, brutal obsession with the seizure of political power. There can be little doubt that, when the Spanish Communists began their evolution away from Stalinism (and more recently Leninism) in the late 1950's and early 1960's, many of the changes made in the ideological perspectives of the PCE obeyed a primarily tactical imperative. Over the course of the last twenty years, those ideas developed and assumed a more permanent and strategic dimension. But, while we should not underestimate either the extent or the sincerity of those revisions, there are certain aspects of that evolution which are incomplete and could therefore stand clarification.

One such question relates to the role the Communist party expects to play in the revolutionary process in Spain and to its future relationship with other political and social forces. The contemporary Spanish Communist view emphasizes that all the parties engaged in the construction of socialism would be on an equal footing. Agreed on the fundamentals, they would be free to carry on a lively ideological debate with respect to the best specific measures to adopt at a given moment. At this level, then, the PCE appears to have put aside the Leninist notion that a vanguard role in the Spanish revolution belongs ipso facto to the Communists and that other organizations, if allowed to exist as in the German Democratic Republic or in Czechoslovakia, were to be conceded a clearly subordinate role. The Spanish Communists have opted instead for the more flexible but perhaps no less substantively elitist formulation (like that of the PCI, it draws heavily on, but nevertheless diverges significantly from, the original Gramscian concept of hegemony as equivalent to the dictatorship of the proletariat) which argues that the Communist party has to earn its leading role.[27] It was in keeping with this theme, for example, that Santiago Carrillo generally avoided using the 'vanguard' catch-phrase in his most ecumenical work, "Eurocomunismo" y Estado.

Another doctrinal innovation presented by the Spanish Communists--this one is original to the PCE-- referred to how the alianza de las fuerzas del trabajo y de la cultura (AFTC) would exercise its future hegemony over and within Spanish society. The standard Leninist view emphasizes the Communist party role in that enterprise. The PCE does likewise, but it insists that the vanguard role in the revolutionary process in Spain belongs not to any single party but to the coalition of forces--parties, trade unions, neighborhood and housewife associations, and even a group like _Cristianos por el Socialismo_-- which are grouped in something called the _nueva formación política_.[28] The NFP leads and in some senses coincides with the new historic bloc whose objective is the construction of socialism. It would elaborate a minimum program and establish joint deliberative organs but individual groups or parties would retain organizational autonomy.

Rhetorically, then, the Spanish Communists moved away from the notion that the Communist party is _the_ vanguard of the working class and has a scientific method rooted in Marxist-Leninist ideology which gives it exclusive power to understand and, in some ways, to control the historical process. The change was not without its ambiguities, however. Carrillo and his associates continued to insist on a special role for the PCE. Indeed, they were less than reassuring about their hegemonic intentions (or lack thereof) when they cited the Popular Front as the prototype of the _nueva formación política_ and, more startling, as a situation where there was "a permanent and free contrast of opinions."[29] What is more, all one has to do is read official PCE publications--those of members of the Executive Committee like Jaime Ballesteros, Ignacio Gallego or Nicolás Sartorius and of provincial and regional PCE organizations--to find repeated use of phrases identifying the party as "the vanguard of the working class," as "the political representative of the proletariat" or as "the most conscious part of those masses organized for the political struggle."[30] That such claims are still being made despite the passage of time and the innumerable errors committed in the name of historical clairvoyance suggests that, as far as the Spanish Communist party is concerned, the old dogmas have not just faded away.

The Communist attitude toward the labor movement is a case in point. Contemporary PCE doctrine rejects the classical Leninist 'transmission belt' formulation of party/trade union relations and instead insists that mass movements have to be independent of and autonomous from all political parties. But the Spanish Communists have a peculiar understanding of what "independence and autonomy" mean. For example, Nicolás Sartorius in his book _El Resurgir del Movimiento Obrero_ bluntly stated that "the autonomy of the labor movement is only real if there exist worker parties and if these fulfill their leading role."[31] Certainly, the PCE was not as forthrightly disdainful of mass movements as Lenin

97

in <u>What is to be Done</u>?, but the theoretical prism through which it approached labor still had as a fundamental premise the rather condescending view that such movements (and more generally the working class) were objects into which "consciousness" had to be instilled. Sartorius, to take the most prominent syndical ideologue of the party, could write about the "eminently dialectical" relation which needed to be established between party and trade union, but as Carrillo noted, when push comes to shove, "Communists active in <u>Comisiones</u>, whether at the base or in leading bodies, owed themselves to the party."[32]

Spanish Communist practice in the labor movement did little to erase the doubts those statements raise about whether or not the PCE still has a largely instrumental approach toward the working class. For example, the <u>Comisiones Obreras</u> (CC.OO.) emerged in the early 1960's as a movement based on factory assemblies whose militants took advantage of regime-sponsored syndical elections to infiltrate the official <u>Organización Sindical</u>. This mixture of legal and illegal work, which only the Communists among the more traditional forces on the Left encouraged, helped the movement deal with the rigors of repression. By the latter part of the decade, the CC.OO. had emerged as the principal labor organization in the country. At that time, the Communists argued that the <u>Comisiones</u>, because they were a <u>movimiento sociopolítico</u> which was above political parties, could eschew traditional labor union structures with their bureaucracies and membership rolls. They continued to make this argument until mid-1976 when it became apparent that the CC.OO. would not be able, as the Communists had hoped, to force the dismantling of the vertical syndical structures or take over the <u>Organización Sindical</u>.

It was in this context that the General Assembly of the <u>Comisiones</u> met in July 1976. During that session, the Communists abandoned a decade-long policy and pushed through a motion calling for the transformation of <u>Comisiones</u> structures and the creation of a <u>confederación sindical</u> along rather traditional lines. The change in policy, they stressed, came in response to continued Socialist opposition to the <u>Comisiones</u> and to the fact that Franco's heirs were giving preferential treatment to the Socialist UGT in an effort to lessen Communist strength. These objections or explanations do have a basis in fact, but it can hardly be overlooked that the fundamental reason for the change in Communist policy was that PCE leaders, seeing their drive for syndical and political hegemony on the Left in the post-Franco era thwarted by the continued presence of rival trade union organizations like the UGT and USO, believed the transformation of <u>Comisiones</u> to be the only way the party could effectively compete with its rivals.

Another place where the ambiguities of the Spanish Communist evolution are clearly visible is in the analysis the PCE makes of the character and origins of the Soviet state. To raise this issue may appear at first to be a red herring and its answer to be a point of narrowly historical or academic interest. Nothing could be further from the truth, however. The way the Spanish party responds to those issues reflects its own priorities and the vision of the socialist society which it has. Globally speaking, there are in the Marxist scheme of things five approaches to be taken in analyzing the class content of Soviet society. In shorthand fashion, those options are: state capitalist, neither capitalist nor socialist (a new, entirely unique model of property relations), a transitional society between capitalism and socialism, a primary socialist society and, finally, a fully developed or "real" socialism. Advocates of the last three postures may be found in the PCE. Some in the leadership (old-timers like Dolores Ibárruri, for example) and older sectors of the party base undoubtedly consider Soviet society to be an example of mature socialism. A second group could be said to include various members of the Executive Committee--Ignacio Gallego or even Simón Sánchez Montero--who consider the Soviet Union, despite its errors and shortcomings, to be a socialist society. Gallego considers it better than any capitalist country and Sánchez Montero notes that, except for some bureaucratic deformations, exploitation of man by man has ended there.[33]

The most critical comments have been made--one dare not decide whether out of nationalist pique, democratic conviction, for public relations purposes, or some combination of all three--by PCE Secretary General Santiago Carrillo and Manuel Azcárate, the principal party theoretician and ideologue. In "Eurocomunismo" y Estado, Carrillo argued that the Soviet Union finds itself in an intermediate phase between capitalism and socialism, in a situation analogous to that of the absolute monarchies during the transition from feudalism to modern parliamen-

99

tary democratic practice.[34] As a consequence, both party and society in that country need "a serious and profound transformation in order (for Russia) to become an authentic workers' democracy."[35] Carrillo was ambivalent about the nature of transformations required there, however. At one point in the book, he declared that the _material_ conditions for passage to a _socialismo evolucionado_ had been fulfilled; at another, that fundamentally important political _and_ economic problems were still on the agenda.[36] Azcárate, for his part, has argued that 'primitive socialist' relations of production exist in the Soviet Union but that an authoritarian State keeps many features of capitalism and repression.[37] What neither one of them rejects is the opinion that the Soviet State created in the wake of the October 1917 revolution was not only of historical importance but, despite its subsequent shortcomings, well worth the price.

That, despite everything else they have written, Spanish Communist leaders continue to idealize the Bolshevik seizure of power is readily understandable, particularly if we remember how the roots and identity of the PCE are and have been bound up with the October revolution. For whatever reason, Carrillo, the most legitimate claimant the international Communist movement has to the role of Martin Luther, has demonstrated himself unwilling to renounce that patrimony. But when he continues to insist that Lenin and the Bolsheviks should have seized power, he and his party assent to the notion that socialism, at least in its lesser forms, does not require political liberties. They are, in effect, holding to the view that socialism and democracy do not necessarily go hand in hand, that "when a revolutionary _coyuntura_ develops, one has to take advantage of it and seize power."[38]

Further questions arise when we consider the Spanish Communist position on the violation of human rights in the Eastern bloc. Since the mid-1960's, the PCE has repeatedly criticized what it has termed violations of 'socialist legality' there. The first thrust in that direction came in 1966 with the publication of an article by Carrillo decrying the imprisonment of Soviet dissidents Daniel and Siniavsky.[39] It was followed up in subsequent years: the Spanish Communists objected in 1974 to the measures adopted by the Soviet regime against Alexander Solzhenitsyn and in 1977 they protested the jailing of the signatories of Charter 1977 in Czechoslovakia.[40]

One might conclude at first glance here that little more could justifiably be asked of the PCE on these occasions. Upon closer inspection, however, one is struck by the peculiar distinctions the Spanish party has made before deciding whether or not to criticize human rights violations and political repression in a 'socialist' country. Thus, the PCE invariably distinguishes between situations where 'socialism' is in danger and where it is not. One particularly demonstrative example of this sort of reasoning may be found in the Carrillo book/interview Demain l'Espagne.[41] There, the Spanish Communist leader criticized the campaign directed at Solzhenitsyn but expressed his support for the Castro regime's no less abhorrent treatment of the dissident Cuban poet Heberto Padilla. The distinction between the two cases turned, in Carrillo's opinion, on the issue of how 'dangerous' each writer was to his native social and political system.

The unwillingness of Santiago Carrillo (and we may safely presume his party) to accept the notion that political repression is beyond 'class' and needs to be forthrightly condemned regardless of circumstance is of deep political significance. You cannot have it both ways. Either liberty is consubstantial with socialism or it is not. Either democracy is the only guarantee of socialism or it is not. And if the Spanish Communists do not think that it is, the depth of their conviction about democratic socialism must, to say the least, be brought into question.

IV

So far we have focused on the changes brought about in the Spanish Communist ideological matrix by shifts in the strategic vision of the party. The adoption (at least for the short and medium term) of revolutionary reformism and the shelving of plans for a quick assault on the citadels of power also had an important impact on the structure and the functioning of the PCE.

Organizational practice and ideological belief have always been closely linked in the Communist scheme of things. Joined in a relation of interdependence, both dimensions have helped to establish the distinctiveness of Communist parties. The vanguard claim to historical omniscience which flows from it represented the ideological justification for the maintenance of a highly centralized, quasi-militaristic party apparatus. Equipped with the instrument of democratic centralism, the leaders of that apparatus have been able not only to shift policies radically at times but to stifle dissent.

Most Communist parties did not live up to the 'combat party' ideal type sketched in the famous Twenty-One Conditions adopted by the first Comintern Congress, but they came close enough in the 1920's and 1930's so as to fan a virulent anti-Communist reaction in many countries. Over the course of the last three or four decades, as the Communist movement in Western Europe has had to face up to its inability to conquer power in the region by relying on traditional Leninist methods, there has been a certain softening of organizational doctrine and practice in most of the Continental parties. The first steps away from the Leninist cadre party date back to the Popular Front era when parties like the French and the Spanish attained memberships numbering in the hundreds of thousands. A coherent, alternative doctrine with respect to organization did not really begin to develop, however, until the period following World War II, when the PCI and preeminently Palmiro Togliatti—faced with a tremendous expansion in membership as a result of the Communist role in the anti-fascist Resistance but increasingly conscious of the unlikelihood that any revolutionary explosion would soon take place—laid the foundations for the partito nuovo, a party structured along democratic centralist lines but flexible enough to accommodate and manage a mass-based organization.[42]

The Spanish Communist party, whose development into a mass movement during the Civil War had perhaps encouraged Togliatti in this direction, had by contrast experienced a harsh repression after the Franco victory in 1939 and many of its members either died or went into exile. What remained of the PCE organization in Spain was a reduced nucleus of activists with little organic connection between them besides the Radio España Independiente transmitter broadcasting from Moscow. The unsuccessful guerrilla struggle which the party helped wage in the 1940's further decimated it. By the latter part of that decade, the guerrillas had degenerated into bandit groups, active in remote rural areas but isolated from the general population.

Acting under similar circumstances, the Portuguese Communist party developed a sectarian ouvriériste orientation. The PCE turned inward in the late 1940's, but a changing of the guard in the next decade prevented the hardening of those narrow and dogmatic policies within the party. The renovation began after the death of Stalin in March 1953 and picked up steam at the 5th PCE Congress in 1954 with the entry into the Central Committee of new members who worked in Spain. Its first phase ended in 1956 when Santiago Carrillo and his supporters in the highest ranks of the party--their expulsions from the PCE had been imminent when, fortunately for them, the 20th CPSU Congress with Khrushchev's condemnation of Stalin and his cult of personality and the first truly important political demonstrations in Spain since the end of the Civil War intervened within a few weeks of each other--assumed control of the party. Later we shall discuss in some detail the struggle for power in the PCE in the early and mid-1950's. What is important to note here is that the shift in leadership had important organizational consequences.

Carrillo wanted the PCE to begin laying the foundations for its transformation into a mass-based organization. Accordingly, he supported the modification of party statutes at the 6th PCE Congress in December 1959 so as to permit membership without formal participation in cells.[43] Over the course of the next decade, the party broke organizational tradition further, taking advantage of the protection afforded Communist lawyers, engineers, doctors, economists and the like by the colegios profesionales (professional associations) and permitting the establishment of organizations along essentially corporatist lines. These changes had as their objective not only protecting party members from the hazards of clandestinity but facilitating the incorporation of intellectuals and professionals (representatives of the fuerzas de la cultura) into the party. Another manifestation of the attention the PCE devoted to catalyzing anti-Franco sentiment among intellectuals, in the universities and among professional groups and in attracting them to its ranks was the publication of clandestine journals like Argumentos, Realidad, Revolución y Tecnica and Revolución, Ciencia y Tecnica. It is difficult to assess the success of those efforts. Many intellectuals and university-trained people were at some point either members of the PCE or came under its influence, but only some of them remained in the party for extended periods of time. On the other hand, we still do not know how typical the case of someone like Ramón Tamames is in this regard. He apparently entered the PCE in 1956 and became a member of its Executive Committee in the summer of

103

1976: in between, this prominent economist was a consultant to various ministries and played a role in shaping national economic policies. Aside from the Comisiones Obreras, the PCE also used front organizations like the Movimiento Democrático de Mujeres, neighborhood and housewife associations, and various Clubs de Amigos de la UNESCO, particularly those in Madrid and Alicante but elsewhere as well, to develop contacts with various social strata.

The effort the Spanish Communists made during the years of clandestinity to expand the membership base of their party led to one particularly interesting organizational innovation, the creation of regional Communist parties first in Cataluña, the Basque country and Galicia and later in Asturias, Andalucia, Valencia and in other parts of the country. The idea behind this policy was to take advantage of historical tensions between center and periphery in Spain--Carlos Rama has remarked that fault for the conflict lies with the Castilian monarchs who "did not know how to make Spain"[44]--which had been seriously aggravated by the autocratic centralism of the Franco regime. The results of this policy have been mixed, however. The PCE was not overly successful with this strategy in the Basque country and Galicia. In the first region, the Partido Comunista de Euzkadi had to deal with the presence of extreme nationalists of the various Euzkadi ta Askatasuna groups and the fact that many young people in the region (not to mention their more conservative elders) distrusted the Communists and saw in the PCE little more than a sucursal for the Madrid-based leadership. In Galicia, what strength or presence the Partido Comunista de Galicia had was due to the presence of the Comisiones Obreras in the industrial centers like Vigo and El Ferrol and the party had difficulty penetrating outside the large factories or among peasants in the countryside. It was in Cataluna that the Communists had their most notable success. There, the Partit Socialista Unificat de Catalunya (PSUC), product of a fusion of four groups in July 1936, had a leading role in the constitution of several opposition fronts such as the Assemblea de Catalunya and the Consell de Forces Politiques de Catalunya and, despite the distrust of the most catalanista sectors of the population, became one of the most important groups in the region. Although the PSUC entered the Comintern in 1939--the only regional party ever to do so--and in subsequent years its organization suffered from periodically recurring internal

104

problems over how seriously to take its regional specificity, there can be little doubt that during the Franco era the PSUC functioned primarily as an instrument of the PCE's political strategy and its organizational autonomy was severely limited. In this latter respect, it is worth noting that the negotiations leading to the entry in 1974 of the leftist group called Bandera Roja into the PSUC were carried on by Santiago Carrillo and the regional party leadership was only asked to give pro forma approval to the results. As we shall shortly see, however, things have changed in that respect more recently.

Although beginning in the late 1960's official party spokesmen did not hesitate to claim for the PCE a membership in excess of 100,000 people, it is evident they exaggerated the success of their efforts rather greatly. Even the 160,000 members claimed in April 1977 (or the target figure of 300,000 to be attained by the end of that year which the Central Committee set in July 1976) were far off the mark and exceeded the capabilities of the party. A close reading of the Spanish and Communist press in the last year or two as well as conversations with PCE members leads me to the conclusion that in early 1977 the Communists were lucky if they had 35,000 members. The emigre Communist organization had approximately 7,000 of these. Other important PCE centers were in Madrid (7,000), Barcelona (5,000), and Asturias (3,000). Only after Franco's death in November 1975 can we say that the PCE began to break out of the mold of a restructed partido de cuadros. Even then, the difficulties it faced in many areas inhibited the transformation. The final step in laying the structural foundation for this shift did not in any case come until July 1976 when the Central Committee at its plenary session in Rome instructed Communist organizations to drop the traditional cell structures and change to work and neighborhood agrupaciones which would hold public meetings. Another important step in this respect came on the crucial issue of defining the rights and obligations of party membership. Thus, Santiago Carrillo in his report to the Central Committee talked about the necessity of accepting varying degrees of involvement in party life and of a party composed of adherentes, militantes, and cuadros.[45]

The implications of the shift from cell to agrupación along with those related to the expansion in the number of individuals in the leading bodies of the party and in the party more generally have

105

not been altogether clear. On the one hand, the various decisions aimed at creating a mass-based party represented a clear break with the Leninist tradition and were an important step in the de-militarization of the party. On the other hand, a growth in the number of people in an organization does not necessarily make it more internally democratic or less anti-democratic in its approach to social and political problems. Brusque policy shifts on the part of the leadership may become more difficult to accomplish during normal times, but such changes hardly assure that during crisis conditions--when, after all, the challenges to democracy are truly great--the party might not opt for a course of revolutionary adventure. The expansions of the PCE Central Committee from 40 members in 1965 to 111 in 1970 and 134 in 1976 (its size rivaled that of parties with much greater memberships) does not _ipso facto_ lead to greater democracy within the party. Faced with a Central Committee rendered unwieldy by its numbers, the important decisions continued to be made by a reduced number of people either in the Secretariat or in the permanent committee of the Executive Committee. Predictably, some provincial PCE organizations used the shift from cell to _agrupación_--in the Communist jargon this was known as _territorialización_ and it affected primarily service sector employees organized by _ramas de producción_ and professionals in the quasi-corporatist _agrupaciones_--to strip power from troublesome elements. Thus, in Madrid, the provincial leadership associated with Executive Committee member Victor Díaz Cardiel dissolved the highly politicized and critical lawyers' _agrupación_ blasting the undue influence professionals and intellectuals had in the _dirección política_ of the party and warning of the risks this entailed for the 'de-naturalization' of the PCE.[46] Those who expected the decision to _territorializar_ to bring about radical changes in the attitudes and patterns of the PCE were to be disappointed: party leaders were quick to clarify that work-place _agrupaciones_ were preferable to neighborhood ones and that the functions of the cell had not been abolished but rather shifted so as to become the responsibility of the _comite político_ of the _agrupación_.

## V

The decision to transform the PCE into an authentic _partido de masas_ went hand in hand with promises of greater internal democracy and freedom of discussion. As we shall see, it is not clear those promises have been fulfilled but what cannot be denied is the fact that, over the course of the last three decades, the Spanish Communist Party has become much more open and discussion, although circumscribed, takes place in its ranks to a degree unequalled in its history.

The distance travelled by the PCE in this regard should not be underestimated. In the 1940's and early 1950's, disagreement with or disobedience of the directives emanating from the Political Bureau (as the highest policy-making organ in the party was called until 1960) brought with it the very real threat of physical elimination. The decade and a half after the end of the Civil War was a rather sordid chapter in Spanish Communist history and it is small wonder that those members of the present leadership who lived through the period make few references to it.[47] Most of them had emigrated in 1939 to the Soviet Union and their personal squabbles and petty conspiracies over who would inherit the post of Secretary General from the deceased José Díaz--he died under somewhat mysterious circumstances in 1942 in Tiflis--became enmeshed in the cloaca of Stalinism. The Communist exile community in the Soviet Union and Eastern Europe was a particular target of the KGB and, at one point, some of the leading figures in the PCE were nearly charged with plotting against the life of Dolores Ibárruri.[48] She was more than once rumored to have been arrested by the police in the late 1940's. The exiles set their quarrels aside only when they felt challenged by those considered to be outsiders. For example, they expelled Jesus Monzon, accusing him of "deviationism and adventurist opportunism," after he resisted their efforts in 1944-45 to reassert control over the clandestine Communist organization in Spain.[49] His was certainly not an isolated case. Spanish Communist guerrillas, acting under instruction from the leadership, executed a dissident Communist leader, León Trilla, in 1945.[50] Joan Comorera, the first Secretary General of the PSUC, and other Basque Communists tried to break the control exercised over their respective regional parties by the parent PCE organization, and for their trouble were expelled in 1948 and accused of being Titoists. At the height of the campaign against Comorera, the clandestine Communist transmitter Radio España Independiente, in what was tantamount to a death sentence for someone living in

107

Spain, accused him of "being openly at the service of the Francoist police and serving in the repugnant role of informant."[51]

The search for and condemnation of 'agents' in Spanish Communist ranks came to an end for the most part with the death of Stalin. Party leaders attributed their mistakes and crimes to the excesses of that Soviet leader and to Beria. Over the next few years, as in most other parties, the struggle between rival factions in the leadership which had been going on for several years in relatively muted fashion broke out more and more into the open. It was more than anything else a generational struggle, pitting younger members of the leadership who had joined the party in most cases just prior to the Civil War--men like Santiago Carrillo, Fernando Claudín, and Ignacio Gellego--against older stalwarts like Vicente Uribe, who directed clandestine party activities in Spain, and Francisco Anton, whose rise in the leadership had been directly related to his close ties with Dolores Ibárruri. Because of her symbolic importance--she was also Secretary General--she stood in many ways apart from the fray but could not have been very comfortable during her speeches to party cadres when she admitted to serious deficiencies and sectarismo in the work of the leadership.

Self-criticism was, in any case, entirely appropriate. The party stood in splendid domestic and international isolation. The Central Committee had not met in plenary session since the Civil War. And the exiled leaders were too busy enlarging their respective fiefs and plotting against each other to devote much time or effort to the anti-Franco struggle. The inner party jostling continued during the 5th PCE Congress in September 1954 with the previously noted entry of new members into the Central Committee and the ouster of Anton from that body and the Political Bureau.

As we have discussed elsewhere,[52] matters finally came to a head in late 1955 with the admission of Spain to the United Nations. Against the majority of leadership and in a breach of party discipline, Carrillo argued in an article published in Mundo Obrero that the PCE should drop its opposition to the move and devote its efforts to strengthening the anti-Franco opposition within Spain. On the verge of expulsion, Carrillo and his supporters escaped that fate when the results of the 20th CPSU Congress became known and important opposition political and labor strikes developed in Spain. Dolores Ibárruri, more than capable of sensing which way the wind was blowing in the Soviet Union, then decisively shifted her support to Carrillo and those who argued for more open and adaptive policies. Carrillo would not be elected Secretary General until the 6th PCE Congress in 1959 (with Ibárruri elevated to the largely honorific post of party President), but by the spring of 1956 he had assumed a dominant role in the affairs of the party. At a special Central Committee plenum called in August 1956 to ratify his ascendance, he lashed out openly at Uribe for his "anti-democratic methods" while insisting that the deformations brought about by the cult of personality had nothing to do with democratic centralism as the guiding organizational principle.[53] In all of this, one of the most remarkable developments was the ability Carrillo demonstrated--something he shared with Khrushchev--to maneuver so that his own past role and excesses were not too great a liability. Although a young man, Carrillo had been a prominent figure in the PCE Political Bureau in the 1940's and--while lucky never to have lived in Moscow for any extended period of time--certainly had his share of soiled laundry.

The changes in policy Carrillo made after assuming a dominant position in the PCE went against the grain of many Communist militants and provoked serious internal strains. Real disillusionment did not set in until the early part of the next decade, however, when it became apparent that predictions about the imminent downfall of the regime were far off the mark. Earlier in this chapter, we discussed the exodus of many younger and some older militants and their decision to form a multiplicity of extreme Left groups. Repeatedly, and to some extent justifiably, alluding to the dangers too open a discussion would bring, Carrillo did not hesitate to use his control of the party apparatus and the device of democratic centralism to silence those who refused to accept the new line.

Even as influential a member of the PCE Executive Committee as Fernando Claudín could not break the hold Carrillo exercised over the Spanish party. Earlier, we discussed some of the differences he and fellow Executive Committee member Jorge Semprún had with Carrillo and there is no need to discuss the matter in detail here. Suffice it to reiterate that by 1963, after the failure of the huelga nacional to materialize, he had developed a rather distinct alternative conception of the via española al socialismo premised on the notion that the Franco regime would probably evolve into a Western European-style parliamentary democracy. The discussion over this

109

and other points Claudín raised (such as greater internal democracy and independence from the Soviet Union) lasted well over a year but, at a March 1964 Executive Committee meeting, Carrillo and his supporters refused to accede to Claudín's demands that a special Central Committee meeting be called to debate the issues and dismissed the dissidents from their posts. Formal expulsion came a year later.

That Carrillo exhibited a certain tolerance toward Claudín and Semprún and permitted a more or less open debate at the highest ranks of the party (that is, among the members of the Executive Committee) was due in part to the fact that both men were known for their intellectual and personal honesty and that neither looked for outside sources of support or used the issues raised as a pretext for setting up a rival organization. More importantly, however, the two men had been among the strongest supporters Carrillo had had after 1956 and held important posts within the party. While trying to avoid too sharp a clash with them, he also had to take care not to appear too closely identified with them lest disgruntled older members of the leadership take the occasion to blame Carrillo for moving too fast since 1956 and not knowing how to keep a handle on the situation. What brought Carrillo and those older party leaders together was an aversion to have power slip out of the hands of the exiled leadership. The demand Claudín and Semprún made about having a plenary meeting of the Central Committee called to discuss their views and their insistence on a full debate throughout the Spanish Communist organization was unacceptable.

Whether Claudín and Semprún could have gained the support of a cadre base whose members were getting tired of being constantly exhorted to bring about the illusory huelga nacional is, of course, impossible to ascertain. Whatever the merits of their arguments, it would probably have been exceedingly difficult, from a psychological point of view, for many Communists operating in Spain to have accepted as a given the failure of their longstanding efforts to overthrow Franco. In any case and whatever his reasons, Carrillo forced the suspension of Claudín and Semprún from their posts in the Executive Committee and then opted at an April 1964 meeting of cadres in the Parisian suburb of Stains to violate a tacit agreement not to discuss the issues in public until the Central Committee had had a chance to ratify that suspension by openly attacking the two men.[54] He rejected their demands for a general discussion and the distribution of the rival platforms. In early 1965, coinciding with the announcement of their expulsion, a Claudín text was published in the theoretical journal, Nuestra Bandera: it was in small print with an official rebuttal in much larger letters interspersed through the pages. As it turned out, many of the Claudín/Semprún arguments and views were subsequently incorporated into the PCE program by Carrillo and there is a good deal of substance to the charge made by those men that they were the first and most authentic Eurocommunists in the Spanish Communist party.

Carrillo handled the challenge posed by pro-Soviet elements after the Czech invasion with no less dexterity. Conscious of how reflexively pro-Soviet most party members were--the anecdote is told and it may well be true that immediately after learning that Warsaw Pact forces had entered Prague, Marcelino Camacho who was in jail at the time convened the group composed of Communist party members and sympathizers and explained why the intervention had been necessary; shortly thereafter, he learned of the decision taken by the Executive Committee and rectified the mistake--and unsure of how committed Moscow was to 'normalizing' the situation in the PCE, Carrillo was at first cautious. Eduardo García, the Organizational Secretary, and several other members of the Central Committee opposed the official line, but he remained at his post for nearly nine months, being ousted only after circulating an Open Letter criticizing Carrillo and the decision to break ranks with the Soviet Union among émigré groups.[55] Similarly, Enrique Líster, who was responsible for international affairs and had been in close contact with the Russians since the invasion, was expelled only after months of haggling and negotiation. Through the months after 1968, Carrillo used the increasingly open fractional activity which the dissidents engaged in as a way of rallying the leadership and the cadre base behind him. He did not yet voice the biting criticisms of the Soviet Union, of its domestic and foreign policies, that would become his trade-mark in subsequent years; and, instead emphasized the negative consequences such fractional activity would have on effective anti-Franco action. Such arguments carried a lot of weight, particularly as they were reinforced by decades-long tradition of more or less unthinking submission to orders emanating from the top. Dolores Ibárruri played an important role in this affair. Known for her close ties to Moscow, she nevertheless opted at a critical moment to side with Carrillo. That decision by and large settled the issue for the pro-Soviet faction; although Carrillo, just to be on the safe side, had the Secretariat coopt 29 new members to the Central Committee prior to a September 1970 showdown with Líster.

Carrillo survived the threats to his leadership cited in the preceding paragraphs (as well as numerous other less important ones posed by Marxist-Leninist groups and the OPI in 1973 and 1974) through judicious use of democratic centralism and the organizational instruments it supplied. Democratic centralist principles like the submission of the minority to the majority will (that is, not simply accepting the decision but actively supporting it down the hierarchical line), the interdiction of horizontal communications between potential or actual minorities in different cells or other party organs gave the leadership great leeway in handling dissent. Party statutes--particularly articles 13 permitting unlimited cooptation into and by the Central Committee, 21 allowing that body to establish the norms for selection to the party congresses, and 26 permitting the designation of any members of lower party organizations by the Central Committee--also helped in that endeavor.[56]

When speaking about internal democracy, party leaders inevitably insisted that a strict centralism was necessary under conditions of clandestinity. Once the party were legalized and operating openly in the country, a much greater discussion would be encouraged. It would have limits, of course. Democratic centralism would still be the guiding or organizational principle and, although it would function with a greater emphasis on the 'democratic' than on the 'centralism,' currents of opinion would never be permitted to take organic form and crystallize into factions.[57]

The rationales offered by the PCE leadership on the necessity for democratic centralism and its continued viability despite changes in ideology and political strategy varied, but they generally revolved around two notions. One of these was that the existence of factions was tolerable or natural only in a multi-class party and not in the party of the working class whose political homogeneity had to be maintained. The other, that as the fusion of revolutionary will and action, the PCE could not, as Santiago Carrillo said in Demain l'Espagne, "permit itself, through an excess of democratisme, to lose the opportunity to act."[58]

112

Both of these ideas (and this is something touched upon earlier) point up an essential ambiguity in the organizational/ideological evolution of the PCE. Centralization of functions and homogeneity in the party can hardly be said to deepen its democratic quality. Certainly, it is true, as Communist leaders repeatedly insisted, that in some respects other Spanish parties functioned as centralistically (or oligarchically) as the PCE, but the crucial difference between the Communist and most other parties resided then and now in the fact that the latter did not have globalist aspirations to bring about radical--in the sense of profound-- changes in society. The argument in favor of separation and balance of powers in the party and outside it as well as the idea that no class or group can honestly make a claim to be the fountainhead of all worthwhile ideas may be profoundly liberal notions but they are also deeply democratic ones. Just as there is no way around having the way you come to power spill over into how you exercise governmental responsibilities, so there is no way to construct an aritficial barrier between what is prized in terms of internal organization and political or administrative choices for the society at large. It has been rather incongruous, in fact, for PCE leaders to insist with such vehemence on diversity and the propriety of 'national' paths with respect to the international Communist movement and to then turn around and praise a model of internal organization which enshrines quite an opposite ideal.

In only one Spanish Communist organization-- the Partit Socialista Unificat de Catalunya--has democratic centralism been sufficiently watered down so that authentic political debates and a lively competition among different groups could take place.59 The internal democratization of the PSUC picked up in the twilight of the Franco era and the party, perhaps not so coincidentally, turned in a rather good performance in June 1977, receiving nearly 18 percent of the vote in the four Catalan provinces. There are, of course, any number of reasons which may be adduced to explain the PSUC vote, but all are insufficient if they do not take into account the fact that the Catalan Communists were able to convey to the electorate the image of an open and socially heterogeneous party. That image is not far from the reality of Catalan Communism and, at times over the last two years, the situation in the PSUC has been volatile. Divergences

113

within its 75-member Central Committee were so intense that they forced the postponement first of a Barcelona provincial conference and later of the Fourth Congres of the party, originally scheduled for the spring of 1977 and finally held in November of that year.

There has been a sharp lucha por el poder (struggle for power) going on within the PSUC between several groups. One of these can generally be identified with individuals who had been in the splinter leftist group known as Bandera Roja and who had entered the PSUC in late 1974. Although BR had been very much a radical, leftist organization in the late 1960's and early 1970's, some prominent representatives of this current like Jordi Borja, Alfonso Carlos Comín and Carlos Navales--Jordi Solé Tura is also a former member but he is much closer to Carrillo than the others--have come to be regarded since their entry into the Communist party as members of the 'social democratic' wing.[60] A second faction, rallying around former Secretary of Organization Josep Serradell and Margarida Abril, also of the PSUC Executive Committee, has been dubbed the 'historic' sector. As the name suggests, its most distinguished exponents have been in the PSUC for some years and have a vision marked to some extent by their lengthy clandestine experience. Between them stand a third group which has been more or less in agreement with the 'Eurocommunist' theses presented by Santiago Carrillo, but saw no necessary contradiction between 'Eurocommunism' properly understood and Leninism.[61] The fourth faction--described by some as leninistas puros--was much smaller and its influence derived primarily from the intellectual prestige of Manuel Sacristán, perhaps the leading theoretician in Spanish Communist ranks.

The exact nature of the divergences between the various factions are difficult to identify and these probably were more of style than substance. Whatever the motivation, the struggle between the ex-members of Bandera Roja (or Bandera Blanca, as some wags derisively called them) and the históricos became particularly sharp-edged. The former put less stress on class struggle and the need for polarization politics and eventual working class hegemony in the revolutionary process than the históricos. Borja, in particular, wrote an article in the journal Taula de Canvi in which he virtually said that the working class has no greater a right to demand socialism than many other sectors of society.[62]

114

The históricos, on the other hand, wanted the PSUC to retain as much of the Leninist ideological baggage as possible even while the party developed into a mass-based organization. The two groups also developed competing views on what the Communist party's relationship to the labor movement, neighborhood associations and other mass organizations should be. The históricos saw the PSUC (and the PCE) as exercising a necessarily dominant relationship with respect to these movements, while the ex-BR favored a greater, close to absolute autonomy for them.

It would take the 9th PCE Congress in April 1978--and particularly the now famous Thesis 15 dropping the appellation of Leninist and defining the party simply as a "Marxist, revolutionary and democratic organization"--to spark a similar debate in other parts of the Spanish Communist organization and to show how far the party as a whole still had to go before assuming in plenary form the description of 'Eurocommunist.'

## VI

It is not easy to make a global assessment of the changes wrought by Santiago Carrillo and his associates in the Spanish Communist leadership in the spheres of ideology and organization. On the one hand, we must stress the distance travelled by the PCE. From total ideological/political subservience to the Soviet Union and strict reliance on the Leninist model, the Spanish party moved a great distance in the span of two decades, becoming one of the most outspoken advocates of socialism with a human face and altering its internal structures. And yet, as we have noted during our analysis of statements made by authoritative PCE spokesmen or contained in programmatic documents, the Spanish Communist evolution has not been without significant ambiguities. These ambivalences grew stronger the farther one went down the organizational ladder. Unfortunately--but understandably--we have no survey data available to give us a clearer picture of what the ordinary Communist militant or sympathizer thought about the changes impelled by party leaders during the Franco era, but we can be reasonably sure, indeed almost certain, that talk of civil liberties and emphasis on individual rights found little echo in the lower ranks of the party. Efforts to effect a change in attitude there came up against well entrenched ouvrièriste and sectarian orientations whose strength came from having helped the party survive the rigors of clandestinity. The influence exerted within the party by individuals imbued with these attitudes had been minimized during the 1960's and early 1970's as the PCE concentrated its efforts on recruiting intellectuals and university activists, but it grew markedly in 1975 and 1976 as the leadership leaned on its labor activists for help in transforming the PCE from a cadre-to a mass-based organization.

Although of an obvious, intrinsic political significance, the ambiguities in the Spanish Communist ideological/organizational evolution also had a repercussion on the political ambitions of the PCE. They made it more difficult for the party to cast off its Stalinist past and image (remember here, too, the virulently anti-Communist propaganda emitted by the Franco regime) and thus obstructed the Communist drive for legitimacy, presence and influence in the post-Franco era. So long as the PCE retained its organizational advantage over other opposition groups, this was not a particularly relevant problem. It would become so, however, if the other groups, and particularly the Socialists on the Left, were given the opportunity to flesh out their structures and develop a mass audience. Under these circumstances, the Communist organizational superiority would dwindle and, what was worse, the ambiguities in its evolution would become more the focus of attention. In this sense, it was the Socialist PSOE which, referring to itself as a Marxist and revolutionary organization, posed the clearest challenge to the Communists on this score. We have discussed the political decline and subsequent rise of the PSOE elsewhere. Here, we might simply mention that in the early 1970's control of the party passed to a new generation of Socialist leaders operating within Spain. Battling the Communists for the political space of democratic socialism, the PSOE did not have a Stalinist past and previous embarrassing ties to the Soviet Union to explain away. Its lemma of <u>socialismo es libertad</u> stood subtly but unmistakeably against the Communist one of <u>socialismo en libertad</u>, and the Socialists used widespread popular skepticism about the extent of Communist ideological /political evolution in building a three-to-one lead over the PCE in the June 1977 and March 1979 parliamentary elections. For the Communists, those ambiguities and contradictions remain the most important stumbling block the PCE faces as it tries to build a presence in and to attain plenary incorporation into the Spanish body politic.

NOTES

1. Santiago Carrillo, "Eurocomunismo" y Estado (Barcelona:  Editorial Grijalbo, 1977), p. 23.
2. See the discussion in Guy Hermet, Los Comunistas en España (Paris:  Ruedo Ibérico, 1971), pp. 36-39.
3. Mundo Obrero, July 1956.
4. Corriere della Sera, May 7, 1975.
5. For an early formulation in this respect, see Santiago Carrillo, Nuevos Enfoques a Problemas de Hoy (Paris:  Editions Sociales, 1967), pp. 168-179.
6. Programa Manifiesto del PCE (n. p., n. d.) approved at the Second National Conference in September 1975.  For a more general statement of the economic policies to be followed during the democracia política y social, see Un Futuro para España: La Democracia Económica y Política (Paris:  Colección Ebro, 1967), particularly pp. 119-201.
7. Programa Manifiesto, p. 40.
8. For documents relating to this split, see Fernando Claudín, Documentos de una Divergencia Comunista (Barcelona:  Iniciativas Editoriales, 1978).  A more personal and passionate account may be found in Jorge Semprún, Autobiografía de Federico Sanchez (Barcelona:  Editorial Planeta, 1977).  Sanchez was Semprún's nom de guerre.  The analysis contained in this paragraph relies primarily on those books.
9. Emilio Quiros (Isidor Boix), "Nuevas Características y Tareas del Frente Teórico y Cultural," in VIII Congreso, p. 223.
10. Programa Manifiesto..., p. 31.  Also Santiago Carrillo, Demain l'Espagne, pp. 186 and 189 as well as Después de Franco, Que?, p. 91.
11. Demain l'Espagne, p. 190.
12. Carrillo, "Eurocomunismo," pp. 59-62.
13. Azcárate, op. cit., p. 17.
14. Carrillo, "Eurocomunismo," p. 141.
15. Ibid., p. 103.
16. See the report Carrillo presented to the 8th PCE Congress.  "Hacia la Libertad" in VIII Congreso, p. 81.
17. For an exposition of this thesis, Nicolás Sartorius, El Resurgir del Movimiento Obrero (Barcelona:  Editorial Laia, 1975), pp. 52-87 and 99-113.
18. See the articles "A propósito del libro de

Santiago Carrillo Eurocomunismo y Estado", Materiales, no. 4 (July-August 1977): 5-18; Antonio Domenech, "Crisis del capitalismo, 'eurocomunismo,' perspectiva revolucionaria," no. 5 (September-October 1977): 43-58; and Manuel Sacristán, "A proposito del 'eurocomunismo,'" no. 16 (November-December 1977): 5-14; Julio Rodríguez Aramberri, "La Contradicción del estado burgues," no. 7 (January-February 1978): 7-30. Also in the latter issue, the articles "Sobre Algunos Aspectos del Proyecto de Programa del PSUC" by Francisco Fernández Buey (pp. 31-46) and "Nota sobre la 'alianza de la fuerzas del trabajo y de la cultura'" by Jacobo Muñoz (pp. 47-51).

19. Muñoz, "Nota sobre la 'alianza de las fuerzas del trabajo y de la cultura'," p. 50.

20. Fernando Claudín, Eurocomunismo y Socialismo (Madrid: Siglo XXI, 1977), pp. 119-132.

21. Muñoz, op. cit., p. 50.

22. Cited in Claudín, Eurocomunismo y Socialismo (Madrid: Siglo XXI, 1977), p. 92. The quote is from V. I. Lenin, Collected Works (Sp. ed.), Vol. XXVIII, p. 462.

23. VIII Congreso, pp. 338-39.

24. "Eurocomunismo...," p. 110.

25. Manuel Azcárate, "El Tema de la Libertades Hoy" in Argumentos, no. 1 (May 1977): 14.

26. See Le Monde, July 14/15, 1977 for the text of the one with the PCI and Mundo Obrero, March 10, 1977 for the one from the tripartite summit in Madrid. The proyecto de constitución is in Nuestra Bandera, no. 86 (March-April 1977): 57-59.

27. See, for example, the interview Carrillo gave to La Stampa (Turin), December 14, 1974.

28. Santiago Carrillo, "Eurocommunismo," pp. 129-131. See also his Escritos sobre Eurocomunismo (Madrid: Forma Ediciones, 1977), pp. 84-86.

29. See the introduction Carrillo wrote for José Díaz, Tres Años de Lucha (Paris: Colección Ebro, 1970), p. ix.

30. See Ignacio Gallego, El Desarrollo del Partido Comunista (Paris: Colección Ebro, 1976). Sartorius has claimed the PCE has /see El Sindicalismo de Nuevo Tipo (Barcelona: Editorial Laia, 1977), p. 45/ "the most perfected, scientific and refined instrument for analysis" in Marxism-Leninism. The last phrase in the sentence is from Jaime Ballesteros, "El Partido Comunista en los Umbrales de la Democracia," Nuestra Bandera, no. 85 (n. d.): 15.

31. Nicolás Sartorius, El Resurgir del Movimiento Obrero (Barcelona: Editorial Laia, 1975), p. 76. Also Marcelino Camacho, Charlas en la

Prision (Barcelona:  Editorial Laia, 1976), p. 16
and Sartorius, "Movimiento y Organizacion," Nuestra
Bandera, no. 83 (January-February 1976): 56.
    32. Nicolás Sartorius, El Sindicalismo de Nue-
vo Tipo (Barcelona:  Editorial Laia, 1977), pp. 155-
156.  There may be some controversy over whether my
quote of the Carrillo phrase is taken out of context.
I do not think so.  Here is the paragraph in question:

> The militants of the Party who act in Comisio-
> nes Obreras, although they have a latitude
> while acting in these and trying to achieve a
> unitary synthesis which in each moment responds
> to the collective interests of the workers, are
> not, personally independent of the Party; they
> cannot pay homage to simple, elementary spon-
> taneity, (thus) lowering the role of revolu-
> tionary conscience.  They respond for their
> work to the Comisiones Obreras; but as Commu-
> nists they respond as well to the Party and
> owed themselves to it.  So long as the Party
> does not infringe upon its own principles, its
> own line, with mistaken decisions, there is no
> danger that any conflict emerge between those
> double responsibilities.  If some (conflict)
> does emerge it is because something has failed
> in the labor partidaria which has to be
> checked.

This is from Santiago Carrillo, Hacia el Post-Fran-
quismo (Paris:  Colección Ebro, 1974), p. 76.
    33. Ignacio Gallego, El Partido de Masas (Ma-
drid:  Editorial Cenit, 1977), p. 27 and Simón Sánchez Montero, El Estado (Madrid:  Editorial Cenit,
1977), pp. 17-23.
    34. Santiago Carrillo, "Eurocomunismo," p. 208.
    35. Ibid., p. 212.
    36. Ibid., pp. 105 and 208.
    37. Manuel Azcárate, "El Movimiento Revolucio-
nario Internacional," p. 70 in Tomas Garcia and
Manuel Azcárate, Temas de Politica y Sociedad:
Cuestiones Internacionales (Madrid:  Editorial Cenit
1977).  See also Azcárate, "Problèmes et Perspectives de l'eurocomunisme," Taula de Canvi (Barcelona), Extra no. 1 (June 1978):  24-33.
    38. Santiago Carrillo, Escritos sobre Eurocomu-
nismo (Madrid:  Forma Ediciones, 1977), Vol. I, p.
39.  This is taken from the text of a September 1973
Central Committee report.
    39. Fernando Claudín, "The Split in the Spanish
Communist Party," New Left Review (London) no. 71
(November-December 1971):  76.

40. Mundo Obrero, February 27, 1974 and January 19, 1977. The foreign policy bulletin of the PCE, Información Internacional, no. 6 (February 1977): 10-12 has the text of the Charter 1977 document.

41. Santiago Carrillo, Demain l'Espagne (Paris: Editions du Seuil, 1974), p. 146.

42. See the discussion in Franco Ferrarotti, "The Italian Communist Party and Eurocommunism" in Morton A. Kaplan (ed.), The Many Faces of Communism (New York: The Free Press, 1978), pp. 43-47. Also Donald L. M. Blackmer, "Continuity and Change in Italian Communism" in Donald L. M. Blackmer and Sidney Tarrow (eds.), Communism in France and Italy (Princeton: Princeton University Press, 1975), pp. 34-40.

43. See Santiago Carrillo in his Informe del Comite Central (6th PCE Congress, December 1959), p. 99.

44. Carlos M. Rama, La Crisis Española del Siglo XX (Mexico: Fondo de Cultura Económica, 1960) p. 23.

45. See the report Santiago Carrillo delivered to the PCE Central Committee meeting in Rome in July 1976 entitled De la Clandestinidad a la Legalidad (n. p., n. d.) pp. 61-64.

46. The phrase is taken from the opening speech he gave in March 1978 at the Madrid provincial conference at which the author was present. See also the Informe sobre Política Organizativa (n. p., n. d.) presented at the conference, pp. 7-8.

47. One of the few exceptions--aside from Carrillo and his book/interview Demain l'Espagne--is the interview Manuel Azcárate gave to El País Semanal (Madrid), April 2, 1978, pp. 10-13. One reason he consented to questions on this period was to rebut in part the charges levelled at him and others in the Spanish Communist leadership by Jorge Semprún in Autobiografía de Federico Sánchez (1977). Speculation on events during this time is only fueled by Spanish Communist unwillingness to address questions on this score forthrightly.

48. Enrique Líster, Basta! (Madrid: G. del Toro Editor, 1978), pp. 245-49. Lister has become a passionate opponent of Carrillo, so we have to take his accounts with a grain of truth. Nevertheless, the charges ring true given the general paranoia in the Soviet Union in the late 1940's and early 1950's.

49. The phrase is cited in José Borrás, Políticas de los Exiliados Españoles: 1944-58 (Paris: Ediciones Ruedo Iberico, 1976), p. 50. See also the

120

editorial written by Santiago Carrillo in Nuestra Bandera, no. 4 (1950) and quoted in Líster, op. cit. pp. 233-37.

50. Hermet, op. cit., p. 50. He notes that the PCE claims Trilla was a criminal acting under the cover of the guerrilla struggle against Franco. Trilla had been a deputy to Heriberto Quiñones in the early 1940's and there may have been a settling of accounts. See Líster, op. cit., pp. 238-39.

51. The text of the broadcast by Radio España Independiente and other information may be found in Líster, op. cit., pp. 228-33.

52. See my chapter entitled "The Domestic and International Evolution of the Spanish Communist Party" in Rudolf Tökes (ed.), Eurocommunism and Detente (New York: New York University Press, 1978).

53. Santiago Carrillo, La Situación en la Dirección del Partido y los Problemas del Reforzamiento del Mismo (n. p., August 1956).

54. Ibid., pp. 190-94.

55. See the discussion in Chapter 5 of my as-yet unpublished manuscript entitled Communism and Political Change in Spain, MIT, 1979.

56. Estatutos del Partido Comunista de España--Aprobados en su VIII Congreso, 1972 (n. p., n. d.)

57. See, for example, Mundo Obrero, April 11, 1973. There it is said that "fractions lead to nothing but self-elimination in politics." Also Ignacio Gallego, "El Centralismo Democrático en el Partido," Nuestra Bandera, no. 65 (III Trimester 1970): 18-24 and Jaime Ballesteros, "El Partido Comunista en los umbrales de la democracia," Nuestra Bandera, no. 85 (n. d.): 13-18.

58. Santiago Carrillo, Demain l'Espagne (Paris: Editions du Seuil, 1974), p. 121.

59. The best articles on the PSUC to appear in the Spanish press are those by Alfons Quintá in El País (Madrid) and Enrique Sopena in Informaciones (Madrid). I rely on the typology developed by Quintá in the subsequent discussion.

60. See, for example, the article by Borja entitled "Socialistes i Comunistes davant la Democracia" in Taula de Canvi, no. 2 (November-December 1976): 35-51.

61. Joaquim Sempere of the PSUC Executive Committee has an interesting article in this regard in El País, April 21, 1978. See also his "Sobre la Tradició Comunista i la seva Vigencia," Nous Horitzons (Barcelona), no. 36 (October 1977): 7-18.

62. Borja, op. cit., pp. 50-51. During the course of a debate in Barcelona, Borja declared:

The Eurocommunist parties do not want a society which is split into two halves because we do not have a _moral_ _de_ _derrota_. (To have) the organized working class on one side, and capitalism on the other, is to court disaster.
El Pais, April 8, 1978.

63. See my chapter in William E. Griffith (ed.) The Western European Left (Lexington, Mass: D. C. Heath Co., 1980).

122

# 6
# "Les Nouveaux Philosophes" and Marxism

*Michael J. Sodaro*

> What can one do in a country where one
> of the most important bodies of people--the
> glory-laden intellectuals--admire nothing but
> destruction, without having any conception of
> an order which might be able to replace the
> one they want to destroy? I have no answer.
> Intellectuals normally have a critical func-
> tion,...but the critical function becomes sheer
> nihilism when it produces an absolute condem-
> nation of society, without advancing any idea
> of an alternative society...
>
> ---Raymond Aron
> The Elusive Revolution

## OVERVIEW

Marx Is Dead is the portentous title of a book
written by a young French intellectual in 1970.
Under ordinary circumstances, this belated announcement of Marx's demise would not be greeted with much
astonishment. But in the context of French intellectual life, where Marxism often passes as the lin-
gua franca of enlightened discourse, the news came
to many as a profound and disturbing shock. Of particular significance was that the author, Jean-
Marie Benoist, was known as neither an anti-communist polemicist nor as an apoligist for Gaullism.
On the contrary, he was an academic, sharply

---

The author wishes to thank the following for
their helpful comments: Professors Charles F. Elliott, Carl A. Linden, and Thelma Z. Lavine; Ms.
Elke Mathews, and Mr. Mordechai Pinkasovich.

123

critical of French society, and well-versed in the writings of Lacan, Althusser, Foucault and other luminaries of contemporary French thought. Equally important was the timing of the book's appearance. Coming only two years after the tumultuous social upheavals of May 1968, Marx Is Dead[1] served notice that a far-reaching process of reappraisal of those events was already under way among a certain segment of youthful intellectuals who had, in various ways, involved themselves in France's heady days of near-revolution. Over the course of the next several years, the number of these reassessments multiplied. By the late 1970's a veritable intellectual movement seemed to be in the making as a host of erstwhile radicals, some of them formerly avowed Leninists or Maoists, publicly shed their Marxist colorations of 1968 and unleashed a trenchant critique of the Left. With anti-Marxism as their watchword and the events of May as their point of departure, these writers have created a minor sensation in a country where political battles are still waged in the Manichean terms of "socialism" versus "capitalism." Collectively they have become known as "les nouveaux philosophes" ("the new philosophers").

In addition to their frequently strident rejection of many once-cherished Marxist tenets, the new philosophers have a number of other features in common. One is their unabashed hostility to the French Communist Party (PCF). Viewed as a party steeped in dogmatism and unresponsive to the needs of its own constituency, the PCF emerges from the critical glare of the new philosophers as at best an anachronism, at worst a totalitarian danger to French society. Another trait shared by these writers is a similarly strong antipathy towards the USSR and most other communist states. Here the impact of Solzhenitsyn's writings has been crucial. Many of the new philosophers gratefully acknowledge their debt to Solzhenitsyn for opening their eyes to the gruesome dimensions of Stalinist terror, and to its continuation in muted form in the work camps and prison hospitals of the Soviet Union today. Marx may be dead, but his works live on in the gulag. In the words of Bernard-Henri Lévy, one of the most outspoken of the new philosophers, "The Soviet camp is Marxist, as Marxist as Auschwitz was Nazi."

Finally, on a more superficial level, another distinguishing characteristic of at least some of the new philosophers has been their open cultivation of the media. Much has been made in the press of the photogenic good looks of several of these

124

writers, of their trendy dress and their verbal fluidity, all of which they have successfully employed in projecting an appealing image on TV talk shows and in public lecture halls. This is more than just a matter of style. It reflects a genuine sense of mission at work in the new philosophers' message. More specifically, it betrays an identification with the life-style and thought patterns of the new philosophers' single most important target audience: France's bourgeois left. This is the political milieu from which the new philosophers themselves emerged, and it is the one which they are trying most intently to influence. In a peculiarly Gallic display of paradox, the new philosophers' mission may to no small extent be described as épater le bourgeois gauchissant.

Despite these surface similarities, a close reading of the major writings of the new philosophers reveals a variety of outstanding differences among them. Not all of them attack Marx with the same all-encompassing vigor as do others. For some, it is more a question of determining which parts of Marx must be discarded as chaff, and which parts might still be retained or reinterpreted to provide a more adequate guide to social analysis or future political action. Similarly, the analytical methods which the new philosophers bring to bear on their writings vary considerably from case to case. Whereas one writer may approach his subject primarily through a study of nineteenth century German philosophers (André Glucksmann), another employs the conceptualizations of the French psychologist Jacques Lacan (Philippe Nemo), while yet another prefers the terminology of French structuralism as developed by such figures as Michel Foucault, Claude Lévi-Strauss, and Jacques Derrida (Benoist). Frequently one finds a mixture of all these influences in the space of a single volume, and indeed the often gratuitous references to certain nineteenth century philosophers and prominent French academicians of the present day are occasionally carried to the point of sophomoric pretentiousness. In any event, although the new philosophers generally draw on the same pool of intellectual sources, the methodological emphasis tends to differ from one writer to the next. Furthermore, in several cases some of the new philosophers openly criticize others. In sum, the new philosophers should not be looked upon as constituting a coherent group. Their differences sometimes loom as large as the premises (or conclusions) which bring them together. Though there are several new philosophers, there is no "new philosophy."

Perhaps the most intriguing aspect of the phenomenon of the new philosophers, however, concerns the question of where they are to be situated on the left-right political spectrum. Although all of them proceed from fundamentally anti-Marxist axioms (albeit in varying degrees), this does not mean that they have moved to the center or right of the traditional political continuum. On the contrary. As the ensuing analysis endeavors to show, most (but not all) of the new philosophers are as antagonistic to existing liberal democratic institutions as they are to the totalitarian systems they see as the logical culmination of Marxism. The attitude is patently one of "a plague on both your houses." Although the anti-Marxist underpinnings of these individuals have generally drawn the lion's share of what little publicity they have received in the United States,[2] it would be false to conclude that they have embarked on a deliberate rightward shift. Neither right-center liberalism nor even social democracy constitutes the intended destination of the majority of the new philosophers. This being the case, the relevant questions then become: can one place them on the left? and if so, where?

One way of approaching this issue is to ask how far the new philosophers have moved away from the opinions many of them held in 1968, when they either participated in, or sympathized with, the radical activity of the university students. From much of what has been said thus far, one might be led to assume that, by abandoning Marxism, the new philosophers have in recent years taken major strides away from the revolutionary rhetoric that animated the student unrest in May. Such, however, is not the case. Indeed it is the basic thesis of this essay that, by and large, most of the new philosophers have more in common with the radical inclinations of 1968 than with any other identifiable political orientation. What has changed in the interval is not so much their earlier radicalism, but rather their evaluation of Marxism's relevance in defining that radicalism. That is, Marxism is now seen in retrospect to have been an inadequate vehicle for expressing just what kinds of political and social change the students of 1968 were ultimately seeking. At the same time, Marxism's prescribed strategy for achieving revolution is also now subject to attack as irrelevant to modern France. In short, what most of the new philosophers of today are challenging is not the radicalism of 1968, but their former assumption that this brand of radicalism was compatible, if not identical, with Marxism.

To be sure, the very appellation "new philosophers" begs the question of whether what they say is really new, or whether they even merit the designation of "philosophers." Both of these questions will be broached later in this essay. First, however, it is essential for a clear understanding of where they really stand to go back to their political birthplace:  the événements of May 1968.

## THE PARADIGM OF MAY

The political and social turmoil of May 1968 in France involved several crosscurrents of militant activity.[3]  Three of these are particularly relevant here.  First there were the initial student demonstrations at Nanterre and other major universities which aimed primarily at achieving structural reforms in the French university system.  While leftists of various persuasions tried from the outset to escalate these demands into more sweeping calls for political and social revolution, the desire for university reform, at least for purposes of analysis, can be regarded in itself as a separate and distinct issue.  Most importantly, whereas the revolutionaries' insistence on radical social transformations usually issued in diffuse and vague demands for unspecified radical changes in the political and social order, the desire for academic reform was more specific, definable, and (at least theoretically) capable of being fulfilled within the existing institutional framework of French society.[4]

The second type of activity that occurred in May was the massive strike movement that quickly fanned out across the country.  Following the explosion of the student disorders, some ten million French working people went out on strike, and the occupation of whole factories and offices by their employees became commonplace.  While the details of this extraordinary outpouring of mass discontent cannot be presented here, one aspect of the strike movement deserves to be underscored.  Like their counterparts among the students who were initially interested mainly in university reform, the demands of the workers were for the most part limited in scope and programmatic in nature.  That is, they tended to center around specific demands for higher wages, lower prices, better working conditions, and the like.  Even the widespread support among many

127

workers for more radical measures aimed at establishing some kind of workers' control over the workplace were at least specifiable in programmatic fashion.

In counterpoint to all this, the third type of activity that fed into the May upheaval was defined precisely by its non-programmatic nature. This was the extreme radicalism of the militant student activists who became the leading advocates of indeterminate revolutionary change. Actually it is rather difficult to affix a familiar political label to the beliefs of these students, as the character of their movement was really quite new. Although all of them opposed the liberal constitutional order of the Fifth Republic, most were also opposed to replacing it with either another liberal democracy or some kind of authoritarian regime. Although many of them voiced opposition to the state apparatus as such, few considered themselves to be anarchists in the traditional sense. And, although many of these militants, when pressed to explain their design for the future, expressed themselves in what can only be called utopian terms, they had no blueprint for constructing a definable utopia. Indeed, the principal feature of this inchoate radicalism was that it defined itself precisely by its refusal to define its goals. To specify the structure of the new social and political order which was to replace the existing one was deemed in itself an anti-revolutionary act. The totally spontaneous and undirected nature of this new revolutionary process was succinctly summed up in one of the slogans that proliferated in the placards and graffiti of May: "un mouvement se prouve en marchant" ("a movement gets its bearings as it moves along"). For want of a more traditional term, I shall call this type of student activity spontaneous radicalism.

In addition to their refusal (or inability) to clarify their aims, the radicals shared a number of other principles. One was anti-authoritarianism. In addition to having a basically anti-statist bias, many of the spokesmen of the movement reacted strongly against hierarchical structures in any form. Perhaps the best known of the student leaders, Daniel Cohn-Bendit, plainly articulated this view when calling on his fellow students "to struggle against the formation of any kind of hierarchy."[5] Stressing the purely spontaneous and mass-based quality of the revolution, Cohn-Bendit rebelled against the idea of political leadership itself, whether exercised by a party, a trade union,

128

or a charismatic individual. While not all the student militants may have gone this far, certainly they held a common opposition to "oppressive" regimes, whether "bourgeois" or communist in nature, and many shared a romantic belief in the revolutionary capacity of the masses to lead themselves.

An additional aspect of the radicals' stance was their hatred of the French Communist Party. Criticism of the PCF as a bastion of Stalinist authoritarianism was already present in student circles before the May events, but it reached its zenith as the events unfolded. When the party leadership flatly refused to take advantage of the social chaos by seizing power, and even tried to head off the strike movement by endorsing a settlement negotiated with the Gaullist authorities and the <u>patronat</u> (a settlement which the workers quickly rejected), the PCF stood revealed exactly as the students had described them all along: viz., as timid bureaucrats conscious of their stake in the existing order.[6] At least some of the new philosophers' rancor towards the PCF can be traced to their <u>ressentiment</u> at having been betrayed by a party that backed off at the very moment the revolution seemed within reach.

Another characteristic of the spontaneous radicals worth mentioning was their use of Marxist categories. Not all of the militant students actually felt they were acting out Marx's scenario for proletarian revolution, but most nevertheless consciously borrowed concepts, language, and a certain revolutionary elan from Marxism. Even Cohn-Bendit and other advocates of undirected spontaneity employed an unmistakable <u>discours marxiste</u>. The characterization of the enemy as "bourgeois" or "capitalist," the notion of class struggle, the glorification of the proletariat as inherently revolutionary--these and other Marxist ideas, however reinterpreted to fit the radicals' own situation, were part and parcel of their general world view. It was in part this indiscriminate borrowing of Marxist categories which led to a certain confusion over the relevance of Marxism to the 1968 events, a confusion which many of the new philosophers have lately come to recognize.

Of course, not all the student leaders involved in the May uprising were spontaneous radicals of the Cohn-Bendit type. Some were declared anarchists, some Trotskyites, some Maoists, and some flocked to the more esoteric of the numerous <u>groupuscules</u>. What they shared was a dissatisfaction with modern

129

consumer society, a dedication to overthrowing the Gaullist regime, and the utilization of a Marxist vocabulary. In addition, most of these groupings, with the possible exception of the Trotskyites, also tended to emulate the spontaneous radicals' distrust of hierarchy and their faith in the masses. This was especially true of the Maoists.

In this connection it is interesting to note that several of today's leading new philosophers were either broadly defined Marxists or Maoists in 1968. Their identification with these currents of the May movement provides a key to uncovering the elements of continuity in their thinking in the years since 1968. It also serves to highlight the extent to which their thinking has changed since then. To grasp these contrasting patterns of continuity and change, it is necessary to determine how they interpreted Marxism, and what they meant by Maoism, in 1968.

## WHICH MARX? WHICH MAO?

The richness and complexity of Marx's thought provides ample opportunity for ambiguity and selective interpretation. In part this reflects the subtleties of the dialectic. At least three dichotomies of Marxist thinking are of relevance to the way certain new philosophers have tended to approach Marx. The first concerns the function of the state. Was Marx in favor of the state, or was he ultimately an anarchist, forecasting its abolition? The second dichotomy centers on the timing of the revolution. Did Marx foresee an imminent revolution, or did he regard the revolutionary moment as indefinitely postponable pending the full flowering of capitalist development? The third dichotomy refers to the respective roles of determinism and voluntarism in Marx. Did Marx minimize the spontaneous role of the masses when projecting the inevitability of the revolutionary cataclysm, or did he leave sufficient room for human volition? For Marx , these contrasting alternatives are, for the most part, at least theoretically resolvable in their dialectical interaction. Thus he was alternately statist (the dictatorship of the proletariat) and anti-statist (pure communism); optimistic (The Communist Manifesto) and cautious (The Civil War in France) in his evaluation of the proximity of the revolution; deterministic (scientific socialism) and voluntaristic (the role of class consciousness) in outlining the conditions for revolution. Everything depended upon what stage

130

one had reached in the dialectical progression of history. If this schema made for ambiguity, the confusion was compounded in Marx's voluminous writings and correspondence, in which he would stress at times one, at times the other aspect of these three pairings. In any event, several of the new philosophers themselves have deliberately seized on one side or the other of these posited dualities, thus ignoring or writing off their supposed resolution in the dialectical process. Several examples will serve to illustrate their approach.

André Glucksmann is one of the few new philosopehrs old enough to have begun writing books before 1968.[7] He is also the only one (to my knowledge) to have published a comprehensive explanation of the views he held during the 1968 events. <u>Stratégie et Révolution en France--Mai 1968</u>,[8] completed in early July 1968, sets forth in some detail Glucksmann's understanding of Marx's thought, and explains Marxism's connection to the May events. Indeed, on this last score, the young Glucksmann was most explicit. "Not for a century," he wrote, "has a movement so closely resembled precisely the one which Marx had in mind in 1848." And what, precisely, did Marx have in mind? For Glucksmann in his 1968 garb, Marx was fundamentally anti-statist and a protagonist of immediate, popular revolution. Defining the May movement as an example of "<u>dé-étatisation</u>" and popular revolt, Glucksmann cited Marx as the theoretical guide to both these processes. On the one hand, Glucksmann explained away the concept of the dictatorship of the proletariat by characterizing it as a task that occurs <u>simultaneously with</u> the destruction of the state, not as a separate and distinct phase of the socialist revolution. On the other hand, Glucksmann also found support in Marx's writings for the notion that a revolution could occur even before the final development of bourgeois society and the concomitant rise of the proletariat to majority status. While acknowledging that Marx may have been right in positing the necessity of a bourgeois revolution, Glucksmann asserted that this was true only for particular cases, not as the "general law." In general, Glucksmann maintained, Marx held that all revolutions took off from "a general crisis, that is, from a blocked bourgeois revolution." This broad reading of Marx's analysis of the conditions for revolution enabled Glucksmann to describe the May situation, in which the students played such a critical role, as perfectly identical with Marx's prophetic vision. By defining the students as lumped together

131

with the workers in forming the "modern productive forces," Glucksmann managed to stretch Marx's concepts wide enough to include the radicalized youth of France among the revolutionary forces at work tearing down the "bourgeois relations of production."[9]

Needless to say, this exercise in Marxian scholarship involved a rather selective explication of the original texts. Hence it is not surprising that in Stratégie et Révolution, Glucksmann relied heavily on citations drawn from Marx's writing on the Paris Commune which are favorable to the communards, but ignored those counterbalancing passages which criticize the Commune as a premature revolutionary lark condemned by the laws of history to inevitable failure. Glucksmann was just as arbitrary in his interpretation of Lenin. The Lenin he quoted approvingly in 1968 was the anti-statist, utopian Lenin of State and Revolution. The more disciplined, authoritarian Lenin of What Is To Be Done? Glucksmann dismissed as relevant only to the conditions of Tsarist Russia, not to those of modern France.[10]

It is quite another Marx who emerges as the antagonist in Glucksmann's principal work as a new philosopher. In Les maîtres penseurs (The Master Thinkers), Marx is now villified as...a statist! "Marx and Engels," he tells us, "displayed a penchant for a statist and dictatorial strategy of the proletarian revolution."[11] Indeed, Glucksmann's thesis in this weighty volume is that Marx shared with three other German "master thinkers"--Hegel, Fichte, and Nietzsche--such an overpowering statist bent that all twentieth century manifestations of antisemitism, police states and totalitarianism derive from it. Marx is especially culpable in this regard. Glucksmann the new philosopher assures us that Marx was incapable of conceiving of people or classes outside of the institution of the state, and indeed must ultimately bear responsibility for Soviet Russia's labor camps.[12] Glucksmann even throws water on Marx's fervor as a revolutionary. Marx never wanted a spontaneous workers' resistance to capitalism, he says; "such was not his design." Finally, Marx's insistence on the "scientific" control of historical forces effectively closed the door to the play of voluntaristic revolutionary activity.

Quite clearly, Glucksmann is engaging in a certain exegetic sleight of hand. As if by revolving-door magic, the anti-statist Marx who dominated Stratégie et Révolution suddenly disappears from

132

Les maîtres penseurs, where another, totally different Marx is summoned before our eyes. In neither of these works does Glucksmann take sufficient account of the dialectic as the source of these double manifestations of Marx. For him it is simply a matter of choosing which Marx fits his momentary predilections. One element in Glucksmann's thought, however, remains constant in both his revolutionary guise and his most recent materialization as a new philosopher. It is his anti-statism. Glucksmann's antipathy to the state--any state--runs like a thread through both his earlier and his latest intellectual phases. It is the factor which continues to link him to the student movement of May 1968.

Actually, Marx comes off rather lightly in Les maîtres penseurs when compared with his treatment at the hands of another writer associated with the new philosophers. Francoise P. Lévy, although not usually counted as one of the new philosophers, pursues much the same line of attack as Glucksmann. Her biography of Marx, published in the collection edited by her namesake, Bernard-Henri Lévy (who presides over the publication of a number of works by new philosophers), fires its opening salvo in its very title: Karl Marx, histoire d'un bourgeois allemand.[13] The picture of the "German bourgeois" which Ms. Lévy draws of Marx with slashing strokes resembles few other recognizable portraits of the man. Not only does Marx appear swaddled in his middle class creature comforts and exuding petit-bourgeois prejudices (itself a familiar image conveyed by numerous biographers), but he stands out as supremely uninterested in revolution. As far as Marx was concerned, Ms. Lévy informs us, "the revolution is nothing." By virtue of his social origins, his lifestyle, his personal associations, and above all his theories, Marx comes across as nothing more than a radical bourgeois, for whom the proletariat counted only as an object to be manipulated. His notion that the bourgeois phase of history had to be traversed before one could speak of proletarian revolution is taken as simply the theoretical justification of a lifelong bias in favor of his own class. In Ms. Lévy's acrid portrayal, Marx is a sheer hypocrite, callously insensitive to the sufferings of the working class and "incapable of recognizing the desire for revolution" within it. Especially when confronted with the actual fact of popular uprisings as in 1848 and 1871, Marx is presented as having been passionate in his insistence on the necessity of the bourgeois alliance, often holding back his

133

expressions of contempt for the bourgeoisie until after the revolutionary masses had been safely defeated. She even hints that Marx was a coward for not manning the barricades in 1848 or in subsequent popular insurrections.[14]

In addition to playing the haughty bourgeois, Marx is the object of Ms. Lévy's obloquy for being, among other things, a German chauvinist, an apologist for industrialization, and a sexist. But it is above all his alleged aversion to revolution that draws the author's sharpest condemnation. Significantly, it is precisely this point which brings her back to May 1968. On several occasions Ms. Lévy interrupts her narrative to interject comments about the May events and their aftermath. These are not irrelevant digressions, but reflect an underlying purpose of her analysis. Referring nostalgically in one passage to "what May proposed as possible, as possibility,"[15] Ms. Lévy evokes the fundamental implication of her book: had Marx been in Paris during the tumult of May 1968, he would not have approved. For Ms. Lévy, to be a Marxist is to abandon the revolution.

The role of Maoism in the thought of certain new philosophers presents similar examples of selective interpretation--or misinterpretation. Although no writings by the Maoist contingent of the new philosophers are available from the 1968 period, the books they have published in more recent years reveal that, like Marx, Mao has also undergone a transformation from a revolutionary hero to a foe of true revolution in the eyes of certain French radicals. The two principal new philosophers to have been most overtly influenced by Maoist thought are Guy Lardreau and Christian Jambet. Lardreau's progression from an ardent advocate of Maoism to a more mellowed critic of the Chinese leader is especially transparent, and can be traced in two recent works: Le singe d'or (The Golden Monkey),[16] and L'Ange (The Angel),[17] which he co-authored with Jambet. A comparison of these two books, which were published in 1973 and 1976, respectively, illustrates some of the different ways in which Mao has been perceived by France's generation of 1968.

To begin with, most of the student radicals who declared themselves Maoists in 1968 identified with a particular 'type' of Mao Tse-tung. Theirs was not the authoritarian Mao who had fashioned China into a highly regimented society organized from the top by a party elite. Rather it was the Mao who, by 1968, was convulsing China with the massive purge of the

134

party and state bureaucracy known as the Great Proletarian Cultural Revolution. Thus, when the young French radicals spoke of Mao, they usually had in mind the Mao whose egalitarian ideology and glorification of the masses cast him in the image of an anti-authoritarian liberator of mankind from elitist oppression. The French Maoists' interpretation of the Cultural Revolution was similarly one-sided. In general they saw the phenomenon as an assault on bureaucracy itself, affecting both the party and state elites, and as an attempt by Mao to restore real power to the masses. (Understandably, Mao's reliance on the youthful Red Guards in this operation won particular admiration.) Hence they tended to overlook (or be ignorant of) the extent to which Mao used the Cultural Revolution as a vehicle to secure his own personal power over the party and state apparatus. Both of these interpretations--first of Mao, and secondly of the Cultural Revolution-- squared neatly with the French radicals' image of themselves as anti-authoritarian, anti-elitist opponents of the state, guided only by the spontaneous revolutionary sentiments of the "masses."

Precisely these understandings of Maoism were reflected in Lardreau's earlier work, Le singe d'or. Lardreau started out by asserting plainly Maoism's relevance to the events of 1968. In the May upheavals, "the masses thought" for themselves, thus proving the Maoist dictum that all intelligence comes from the masses. Furthermore, Lardreau maintained, the French masses managed to accomplish this feat without relying on the thought of Marx or Lenin. Lardreau's exaltation of Maoism in Le singe d'or rested on a thorough reevaluation of the significance of Marx and Lenin for modern revolutionary activity. Lardreau deprecated Marx for his "scientific" determinism, which he saw as a barrier to spontaneous action and as responsible for Marxism's degeneration into a series of brittle "laws" of historical development. It was these presumed laws, Lardreau contended, which enabled established communist parties such as the PCF to claim scientific certainty in their interpretation of Marx and to denounce as heretics all opponents of the proclaimed orthodoxy. Consequently, Lardreau proposed in Le singe d'or (which was subtitled, "Essay on the Concept of Stage in Marxism") that Marx's insistence on the necessity of completing various historical stages before proceding to revolution be abandoned. Lenin, for his part, drew fire in this book for advocating the establishment of an elite of party

135

leaders and bureaucratic specialists to run the affairs of the state, with the aim of manipulating the masses from above.[18]

Against Marx's determinism and Lenin's elitism, Lardreau posited Maoism as "the revolutionary thought for our time." Nevertheless, Lardreau did not totally dismiss the contributions of either Marx or Lenin. Both were seen as relevant in many ways to their own time and place. (Even Stalin merited Lardreau's praise in some respects.[19]) Consequently Maoism could not be regarded as completely detached from the Marxist tradition, but rather had to be seen as a new stage in its development. Although Lardreau rejected the determinist Marx, he called for resurrecting the "romantic vision" of Marx as a pure exponent of revolution. In sharp contrast to Françoise Lévy's depiction of Marx as a non-revolutionary, Lardreau felt that Marx possessed an intuitive grasp of the people's desire for revolution, as expressed in his famous phrase, "One has reason to revolt." It was this revolutionary Marx, with his utopian dream of the withering away of the state, whom Lardreau had in mind when he declared, in a candid observation that might have been made by any of the new philosophers, "The whole question is to know, not who, but <u>which</u> will be our Marx."[20] Furthermore, it was this revolutionary Marxism which Lardreau regarded as epitomized today by Mao Tsetung.

Several years later, however, Lardreau had occasion to revise this roseate picture of Maoism's doctrinal superiority. In an essay appearing in <u>L'Ange</u> under the curious title, "Lin Piao as Will and Representation," Lardreau concedes that Maoism has degenerated into an elitist cult of absolute power. The essay is basically an extended comparison of the Chinese Cultural Revolution and early Christian mystical sects, which are regarded as the "cultural revolution" of their own time. Lardreau points out that, whereas both of these enterprises started out with such idealistic intentions as the renunciation of hierarchy, they ended up achieving the very opposite of their original aims. In the case of the Great Proletarian Cultural Revolution, what Lardreau sees as an effort to eliminate power itself ("le maître"--"the master") concluded with the apotheosis of Chairman Mao as the virtual God of the People's Republic.[21] To no small extent, Lardreau's disillusionment with Maoism probably reflected China's foreign policy <u>volta face</u> of 1972, as well as an updated interpretation of the Cultural

Revolution in the light of its subsequent termination. Both of these occurrences made it difficult for western Maoists to assert Mao's aversion to power politics, a fact recorded by a number of French intellectuals, including one of the new philosophers.[22]

In any event, Guy Lardreau's feelings of abandonment by Mao Tse-tung in no way detract from his hopes for a future revolution in France. Together with Jambet, he reaffirms in L'Ange the ultimate victory of an "unprecedented revolution" which will come like an angel to eradicate all oppression at its source by eliminating power itself. With or without Mao, Lardreau and Jambet remain faithful to the radical heritage of 1968.

EAST = WEST

This basic aversion to power in all its forms constitutes one of the few bonds capable of uniting nearly all of the new philosophers, whatever their views on Marx. It provides the foundation stone of their anti-authoritarianism, a position which often expresses itself as an uncompromising rejection of any type of domination by one segment of society over another. Nowhere is this attitude more evident than in the new philosophers' critique of communism. The Soviet Union, its East European allies, and the French Communist Party are the targets of scathing attacks by all of the writers considered in this essay. Whether conceived of as an inevitable outgrowth of Marxist thought, or merely as a subsequent perversion of it, communism as it actually exists is condemned universally as rampant totalitarianism.

Solzhenitsyn has been particularly influential in shaping the attitudes of several of the new philosophers on this score, notably Glucksmann and Bernard-Henri Lévy.[23] Glucksmann has devoted an entire book to excoriating the Soviet system as a "maneater," an epithet borrowed from Solzhenitsyn.[24] Lévy also pays homage to the exiled Russian writer, praising him in almost reverential tones. Both of these new philosophers, moreover, claim that Stalinism and its aftermath represent the logical result of Marx's seminal work. In Lévy's damning phrase, there is "no socialism without camps, no classless society without its terroristic truth."[25]

Other new philosophers are equally critical of established communist states and parties, while differing in their angle of approach. Jean-Paul Dollé, for example, regards Soviet totalitarianism

137

essentially as an aberration of Marxist thought, perpetrated by the arch-authoritarians Lenin and Stalin.[26] For his part, Jean-Marie Benoist takes aim at the Common Program of the French Communist and Socialist parties, denouncing it as a "text of lies." He is especially suspicious of the PCF's professed advocacy of Eurocommunism (i.e., a democratic form of "communism with a human face"), and cites PCF leader George Marchais' recent praise of the Soviet Union as evidence for the party's residual preference for Stalinism.[27] Benoist even took his case against Marchais to the voters in 1978, running (unsuccessfully) against the PCF chief in his home district.

However vociferous in their denunciations of communism, virtually all of the new philosophers are just as critical of western democracies. Glucksmann, for one, claims that the Soviet Union and the United States are both totalitarian systems, hence indistinguishable in their intolerance of dissidents ("contestataires") and their penchant for mass terror (such as the U. S. has inflicted on the American Indians, Japan, Vietnam, etc.). Since Marxism, together with its statist trappings, is essentially western in its origin, Glucksmann sees the Soviet system as merely the projection of West European history onto Russia. His book stigmatizing the USSR as "the cook and the maneater" is replete with comparisons of Soviet brutality with what he regards as equivalent "savage repression" in the West. (To cite one example: Stalin's trial of a hapless collective farm manager in the 1930's is equated with the trial of the Black Panthers in the U. S.) For Glucksmann, the Soviet Union is simply the mirror image of the western experience, "the bolshevik terror is a jacobin-style bourgeois terror." The use of overweening state power to terrorize the Soviet populace is but the realization of a western bias in favor of master-slave relationships in a tradition reaching back to Plato. As a consequence, asserts Glucksmann, "the Russian dissidents can help us know ourselves."[28]

With varying degrees of severity, the other new philosophers also vent their spleen on the West. Jean-Paul Dollé, who of all the new philosophers remains the most wedded to Marxist concepts, denounces the liberal democracies as "commercial societies" ("sociétés marchandes"), in which a bourgeois elite compels the masses to live in misery, ignorance and oppression, and to accept the false values of consumerism.[29] Bernard-Henri Lévy envisages the

138

gradual degeneration of liberal societies into a
"barbaric condition," in which all humanity becomes
"proletarianized" by technological imperatives into
a state of collective helplessness. Even a writer
like Benoist, who placed sufficient credence in the
procedures of liberal democracy to challenge Marchais at the polls, has denounced the French Socialists for being...bourgeois!

To be sure, the term "bourgeois" stands out as
perhaps the highest form of slander available in the
new philosophers' political lexicon. Its applica-
bility arcs widely from left to right, from East to
West.[30] (It never, of course, applies to the new
philosophers themselves.) Together with such terms
as "totalitarian" and "barbarian," the infinitely
versatile designation of "bourgeois" marks the new
philosophers' categorical rejection of all existing
political, economic and social systems. At the same
time, the indiscriminate use of such broadly conceived labels raises serious methodological questions. As employed by most of the new philosophers,
such words as these are intended not merely as handy
epithets, but as tools of analysis. But just how
accurate are they in delineating the political realities which these writers address? It is to this
and other difficulties at the heart of the new
philosophers' reasoning that we now turn.

DISCOURSE ON METHOD

Any effort to ferret out all the methodological
problems embedded in the works of the various new
philosophers would require a far more comprehensive
analysis than is possible in these few pages. Accordingly, all we shall do here is pick out some of
the most salient difficulties in the writings of two
of the more prominent new philosophers: André
Glucksmann and Bernard-Henri Lévy.

As indicated earlier, Glucksmann's recent treatise, Les maîtres penseurs, advances the proposition
that the root of all modern totalitarianisms, whether of East or West, is to be found in the ideas of
four major thinkers: Hegel, Fichte, Marx, and
Nietzsche. The fact that all four were Germans is itself of more than passing interest to Glucksmann.
Nineteenth century Germany is taken as history's
breeding ground of ruthless statism, from whose example the USSR and the United States subsequently
emerged as contemporary imitations. Without delving
into the complex question of the appropriateness of
Glucksmann's linkages between such thinkers as

139

diverse as Hegel and Nietzsche, one is driven to inquire how he establishes the connection between nineteenth century German thought and the political, economic, and social system of, say, the United States of America. In fact the connection is more asserted than demonstrated. As a general rule Glucksmann assumes a far more simplistic notion of the causative impact of ideas upon history than is empirically warranted. His favorite procedure is to select from the profuse writings of the thinkers in question those passages which may be interpreted as advocating such things as a strong state or antisemitism, and then to attribute to these writers full responsibility for all subsequent manifestations of these very phenomena. The word, in short, leads directly to the deed, bypassing all intervening historical variables. Even nuclear deterrence theory emerges full blown from the minds of Hegel and his cohorts among the "master thinkers." There are no curves or detours, only straight lines, in Glucksmann's map of intellectual history.

Bernard-Henri Lévy's Barbarism with a Human Face presents an equally perplexing array of procedural dilemmas. Some of these are definitional in nature. Like most of the new philosophers, Lévy never succeeds in fully defining what he means by such categories as "the bourgeoisie," "the proletariat," "the masses" and the like. This failing only compounds the confusion in his thesis concerning the "proletarianization" of mankind. According to Lévy, the force of modern industrialization and technological advance threatens to reduce all humanity to a single social plateau, which he labels "the proletartariat." Precisely how this will happen is not explained, but that is not the only problem. Lévy describes this universal proletariat as utterly powerless to rectify its status of "generalized servitude." Humankind sinks to the level of increasingly homogeneous "dominated classes." But dominated by whom? If all the world constitutes a single class-- the proletariat--what social groupings are left to impose their domination? Is Lévy suggesting that domination in this state of "proletarian barbarism" ceases to be exericsed by human beings at all, but rather by technical forces? If so, he never specifies in what fashion such a strange occurrence will come to pass. Lévy further complicates his argument by concurring with Ernst Jünger's view that, under these conditions, it is "certain" that class struggles will continue. But which classes will join this struggle if all the world is a single class?

As if this is not enough, Lévy elsewhere in his book certifies that the state as an instrument of domination will never wither away, nor can the elimination of power itself (that elusive goal of the spontaneous radicals) ever be accomplished. On the contrary, Lévy admits, power is the very principle by which all societies are organized. Unfortunately, even though one may accept these premises as eminently reasonable, one is hard put to reconcile them with the postulates of Lévy's proletarianization theses. If mankind in its proletarianized condition is degraded to a uniform position of powerlessness, then who controls state power? And where can one locate this inextinguishable power around which even this erstwhile powerless society is supposedly organized? These and a host of related questions hang in the air, begging for answers.

In addition, Lévy also engages in Glucksmann's questionable practise of drawing arbitrary or spurious connections between historical occurrences and antecedant intellectual currents. If anything, Lévy's sweep is much broader. Not just an identifiable set of "master thinkers," but the entire western enlightenment is to blame for the crimes of Stalin's gulag. Once again, the connecting rods providing the visible spark of contact between these realities are missing. Consequence is confused with subsequence. There is not even the pretense of selective scholarly research to back up these Olympian pronouncements. Clever paradoxes masquerade as settled arguments. Thus, although he is probably the best known of the new philosophers, Lévy is also the most superficial.

WHAT'S LEFT?

Having dismissed as monstrous Leviathans both major political systems of the industrialized world, where do the new philosophers stand on the vital question of what kind of political order should now be devised to replace the existing alternatives? What options are left to them in constructing a viable political strategy for the future? Here again, as in other areas, the new philosophers differ among themselves. In general, however, they tend to arrive at a similar destination via separate routes—although even in this respect one must make certain exceptions. These points of convergence and disagreement become particularly evident in their responses to two questions: what are the new philosophers' attitudes regarding political action? what

141

are their views on the likelihood of a future revolution in France?

With respect to the objectives of future political action, most of the new philosophers who express an opinion on the subject in their books favor withdrawing from traditional political activity altogether, insofar as the aim of politics is simply the taking of power. Bernard-Henri Lévy is categorical in this regard. Never again must intellectuals become advisors to the Prince, he warns, nor should they take it upon themselves to serve the people. The historical record on both these points only shows that, from Plato to Mao, the intervention of intellectuals in the political arena merely reinforces the exercise of repressive power. Consequently Lévy recommends abandoning "politics such as it concretely exists," i.e., the quest for power, and calls instead for devoting one's efforts to "ethics and moral duty." He insists, however, that the obligation to resist "barbarism" in all its forms remains an abiding imperative; only now it is to be fulfilled through strictly intellectual means, such as metaphysics and art. With regard to the second question, Lévy is a professed pessimist. True revolution, he declares, is impossible, precisely because what he sees as the ultimate aim of revolution --the eradication of power itself--is an impossibility. Nevertheless, he maintains that intellectuals still have the duty to at least <u>think</u> <u>about</u> a world from which power has been banished, even though they have no basis whatever for believing that such an occurence can actually come about. Otherwise, without this purely mental exercise, Lévy says that the world would be in even worse shape than it actually is.

Jean-Paul Dollé comes to roughly similar conclusions concerning the futility of seeking power. On the basis of his view that the bourgeois elite exercises its power primarily by imposing its "symbolic order" (i.e. its value system) on the masses, Dollé suggests that the aim of political activity should be to create a new symbolic order from below rather than to change the regime at the top. What he calls for is a "cultural revolution" in the literal sense, aimed at changing basic attitudes towards such things as consumerism, education, art, the family, and even medical treatment from "bourgeois" attitudes to more authentic, mass-based values. Dollé remains optimistic, however, about the chances for revolution. He harbors a profound conviction that "the desire for revolution" continues to smolder in the masses, and,

142

though dormant for the present, it can be coaxed to ignite once again, just as in May 1968.

Guy Lardreau and Christian Jambet are less precise than Lévy or Dollé in delineating a strategy for future action. The same may be said about Glucksmann. Nevertheless, the fundamentally anti-statist inclinations of all three of these writers would seem to preclude any support for activity aimed at exchanging one set of rulers for another. Thus they, too, reject the taking of political power as a legitimate goal of revolutionary activity. Lardreau and Jambet, however, share with Dollé the presentiment that a full-scale revolution, destroying all power relationships in its wake, will one day take place. Without specifying the particulars of this event, they express a deep faith that the "angel" of revolution is surely coming. Glucksmann, meanwhile, is ambiguous and non-committal on this point. Philippe Nemo, for his part, sees virtually all political activity as guided by irrational psychological factors, and regards revolutions as doomed from the start since the revolutionaries, on taking power, invariably behave just like their predecessors.

Jean-Marie Benoist is the true maverick among the new philosophers on these and several other counts. The most critical of the 1968 events, he is also the most outspoken in his support of liberal democracy. In spite of his criticisms of certain aspects of "bourgeois" consumer society, Benoist has opted squarely for western liberalism as against Marxism and communism. Consequently he differs from the other new philosophers by espousing direct political activity. In addition to campaigning against Marchais in the 1978 elections, Benoist has strongly applauded President Carter's human rights policy, and has urged western governments to insist on the strict application of the human rights provisions of the Helsinki agreement by the Soviet Union and its allies.[31] Given these views, Benoist is understandably less interested in the question of political revolution in the West.

With the single exception of Benoist, however, the new philosophers are basically united in their resistance to designing a new political order or even a viable strategy for political change. Indeed, they are <u>against politics itself</u>, in the sense that they oppose the very aim of traditional political action, that of taking power.[32] In essence this consensus on the futility of politics springs from a commonly held belief that power itself is objection-

143

able, and that no real revolution worthy of the name can be considered successful unless it eradicates all relationships of power, whether political, economic, or social. Though they may differ on the question of whether such a revolution is actually possible, not to mention the question of whether Marxism is compatible with such a bold revolutionary aim, these new philosophers share the most radical objective of all: the desire to abolish politics. In this respect, they have moved scarcely a cobblestone's throw away from the young visionaries who dreamed of spontaneous revolution and an end to hierarchy in the streets of Paris in May 1968. It is this radical fundamentalism, at once anti-authoritarian and anti-capitalist, which entitles the new philosophers to occupy a special place on France's political left.

## CONCLUSION

The question now arises as to whether the new philosophers are either new or philosophers. On the first point it would seem that they do represent a novelty, both within the context of French politics as well as on a broader, international plane. Inside France, they have launched the most comprehensive assault on Marxism and the Soviet Union to have emerged from the left in recent memory. Unlike certain leftist intellectuals such as Sartre, at least some of the new philosophers (Lévy, Glucksmann, Benoist) have not been content to limit their criticism to selected aspects of Marx's thought or of the Soviet system, but have insisted that both the doctrine and its historical applications are flawed ab ovo. Others, such as Lardreau and Jambet, have completely jettisoned critical aspects of Marxist thought, and have combined this rejection with a searing attack on Maoist China. While clinging to the anti-"bourgeois" sentiments and political idiom of the French Left, the new philosophers have gone considerably further in detaching Marx and established communism from their leftist attitudes than most of their colleagues at the left end of the French political spectrum. Moreover, the new philosophers seem to have cut themselves off from the main non-Marxist sources of socialist thinking in the French political tradition, as represented by Proudhonism and anarcho-syndicalism. While they have generally not addressed these currents of thought directly, some of the new philosophers have explicitly taken issue with

144

an idea that traces its roots back to Proudhon and his adherents, that of autogestion. The notion that genuine workers' control of the production process offers an effective alternative to both capitalism and statist dirigisme--a view firmly held by many French socialists today--finds little or no resonance among the new philosophers. On the contrary, at least two of them reject it out of hand.33

At the same time, the new philosophers seem to be a uniquely French phenomenon. Few, if any, similar combinations of anti-statism, anti-capitalism, anti-democratism, and anti-Marxism have as yet risen to prominence elsewhere in Western Europe. Even the New Left in such countries as Great Britain, Germany, or the Netherlands is still largely Marxist in inspiration.

The question of whether they are philosophers is a thorny one, if only because few people can agree on an acceptable definition of what constitutes a philosopher. Rather than embark on a tortuous search for an ultimately elusive answer, I would prefer to label the new philosophers political theorists, since they confine themselves to such political matters as the nature of the state, the objectives of political action, and the like. Such a designation, however, is reflective more of the direction of their work than of its quality.

What characterizes most of the new philosophers fundamentally, however, is their general lack of clear answers to the problems besetting the modern world. Rejecting everything, they propose nothing to remedy the conflicts of industrial society beyond a sterile anarchism or a resigned withdrawal into some kind of vague personal moralism. At bottom, most of the new philosophers are radicals without a program, utopians without a utopia. In this respect, they remain loyal to the legacy of 1968. Their acknowledgement of Marx's death casts no shadow over their rejection of "bourgeois" society and its state apparatus. Furthermore, the lessons of Solzhenitsyn have merely reinforced the contempt in which the students already held Stalinism and the PCF in May. The chief discovery of their mature years seems to be that Marx was not with them in 1968 as they had once thought. Mao, too, has turned out to be something less than the helmsman of the revolution he appeared to be then. Bereft of viable political concepts with which to measure the world, the new philosophers--most of them, at any rate--have now turned against politics itself.

145

In the end, what they have to offer is not the consolation, but the poverty, of their philosophy.

NOTES

1. Jean-Marie Benoist, Marx est mort (Paris: Gallimard, 1970).
2. The literature in the U. S. on the new philosophers has been confined largely to newspaper and magazine articles. See, for example, Flora Lewis, "A New Philosophy in France Finds Marxism 'Monstrous'," The New York Times, 31 July 1977; Kenneth L. Woodward and Jane Friedman, "Taking On Marx," Newsweek, 22 August 1977. See also the piece by Eugene Ionesco in the British journal Encounter, entitled, "Of Utopianism and Intellectuals," February 1978, and Melvin J. Lasky, "Solzhenitsyn's Children?," ibid., March 1978.
3. The literature on May 1968 is voluminous. For a partial listing, see Laurence Wylie, Franklin D. Chu and Mary Terrall, France: The Events of May-June 1968, A Critical Bibliography (Council for European Studies, 1973).
4. For more thorough accounts of the student movement, see Alain Touraine, The May Movement (New York: Random House, 1971), and Daniel Singer, Prelude to Revolution (New York: Hill and Wang, 1970).
5. Daniel and Gabriel Cohn-Bendit, Obsolete Communism: The Left Wing Alternative (New York: Mc Graw Hill, 1968), p. 254.
6. For accounts of the students' attitudes towards the PCF, see ibid., and Richard Johnson, The French Communist Party Versus the Students (New Haven: Yale University Press, 1972).
7. See André Glucksmann, Le discours de la guerre (Paris: L'Herne, 1967). The book is a critique of western deterrence theory.
8. The cover of this book shows the title Stratégie et Révolution en France--Mai 1968, but the title pages present the title as Stratégie de la Révolution: Introduction (Paris: Christian Bourgeois, 1968).
9. For the citations and references noted in this paragraph, see ibid., pp. 128; 138; 105; 59; 46.
10. Ibid., pp. 60; 66; 100-101,
11. Les maîtres penseurs (Paris: Bernard Grasset, 1977), p. 107.
12. See ibid., pp. 177; 232. In another recent work, Glucksmann declares pithily that there are "no Russian camps without Marxism." See La cuisinière et le mangeur d'hommes (Paris: Editions de Seuil, 1975), p. 40.

13. (Paris: Bernard Grasset, 1976).

14. See ibid., pp. 312; 283; 253; 260 ff.

15. Ibid., p. 369.

16. (Paris: Mercure de France, 1973). The title comes from one of Mao's aphorisms: "The golden monkey waves his magic wand, and the jade palace is cleansed of dust."

17. (Paris: Bernard Grasset, 1976).

18. For the quotes and references in this paragraph, see Le singe d'or, pp. 25-26; 85-87; 128-129; 134-145; 160-161.

19. Lardreau wrote that the phrase "I love Stalin more than my father" actually meant only "I love the revolution more than anything else," which Lardreau considered an eminently praiseworthy notion. See ibid., p. 161.

20. See ibid., pp. 86-89; 105-106; 132; 161.

21. See L'Ange, pp. 90; 150-151.

22. Jean-Paul Dollé notes that the Cultural Revolution was a "Machiavellian enterprise" undertaken by Mao and his followers to "reconquer a power which they had lost." See Le désir de révolution (Paris: Bernard Grasset, 1972), p. 238N. Among the works by intellectuals in France who have criticized Mao's China, see the following books by Pierre Ryckmans, who writes under the name Simon Leys: Chinese Shadows (New York: Viking Press, 1977) and The Chairman's New Clothes (New York: St. Martin's Press, 1977).

23. A recent television documentary on Lévy and other new philosophers produced by the Canadian journalist Michael Rubbo is aptly titled "Solzhenitsyn's Children." See the transcript of the broadcast published by the National Film Board of Canada. Curiously, the new philosophers do not refer to Solzhenitsyn's attacks on western liberal democracy when attacking the West themselves.

24. La cuisinière et le mangeur d'hommes.

25. See Bernard-Henri Lévy, La barbarie à visage humain (Paris: Bernard Grasset, 1977), p. 184. This book recently appeared in English as Barbarism with a Human Face (New York: Harper & Row, 1979). References here are to the French edition, and the translations are my own.

26. See Le désir de révolution. Dollé's other works include Voie d'accès au plaisir (Paris: Bernard Grasset, 1974) and L'Odeur de la France (Paris: Bernard Grasset, 1977).

27. See Un singulier programme (Paris: Presses Universitaires de France, 1978), pp. 11; 33; 78-79.

28. For some comparisons of the USSR and the West, see La cuisinière..., pp. 11; 22; 93; 96; 97; 102; 111; 136; 210.

29. Dollé even regards birth control as a ruse designed to keep the bourgeoisie from being inundated by a surfeit of hostile multitudes. See Le désir..., pp. 32-33.

30. Philippe Nemo, whose book L'Homme structural (Structural Man) is a bizarre attempt to redefine traditional left-right political categories in terms of phychoanalytical concepts derived from Jacques Lacan, argues that the left is essentially masochistic because it does not really wish to overthrow the bourgeoisie, and indeed behaves just like the bourgeoisie whenever it assumes power, as in the USSR. See L'Homme structural (Paris: Bernard Grasset, 1975), pp. 184-192.

31. See his essay, "Antigone versus Creon," in Trialogue, the bulletin of the Trilateral Commission No. 19 (Fall 1978).

32. On recent tendencies against politics in Europe, see Suzanne Berger, "Politics and Antipolitics in Western Europe in the Seventies," Daedalus, Vol. 108, No. 1 (Winter 1979), pp. 27-50.

33. See B.-H. Lévy, p. 191; Benoist, Un singulier programme, pp. 91 ff.

148

# 7

# Freedom, Marxism, and Modern Man: Solzhenitsyn's Moral Critique

*Charles F. Elliott*

## INTRODUCTION

Solzhenitsyn and Marx both believe that modern man is captive to a condition of false freedom. For Marx, bourgeois society permits only an illusory freedom--the right to be an egoist ("die Freiheit des egoistischen Menschen").[1] This false status has resulted in man's dehumanization and alienation. Man can only transcend this impasse by changing his environment radically through "revolutionary praxis."[2] The bourgeoisie must be destroyed so that the proletariat can transmute itself through the purgatory of "permanent revolution," a dynamic condition ("a harsh and lengthy process," as Marx prophetically hints at the beginning of his intellectual career)[3] which will continue after the seizure of power during the "dictatorship of the proletariat" or "crude communism."[4]

Solzhenitsyn finds man's position at the end of the twentieth century to be as bleak as did the founders of "scientific socialism" in the nineteenth century. There is a "tension and anxiety" in modern man. Modern man suffers a "void /polost!/" within himself and awaits a renewed sense of genuine Purpose.[5] Marx's solution to the problems of egoism and alienation is an external one; that of Solzhenitsyn is a profoundly internal one. Solzhenitsyn, while not denying the reality of the external horrors inflicted upon twentieth-century man, believes that modern man's crisis is one of the spirit. Therefore, it is vain to seek a solution in a changed environment. Instead, there must be a reassertion of the moral worth of the individual and a recapturing of man's true--spiritual--identity which has been lost in the vain pursuit of material happiness and secular self-sufficiency.

149

# FREEDOM, ALIENATION, AND EGOISM

Marx believes that it is necessary (here he blurs inevitability and desirability) that the proletariat (mankind) become totally alienated so that a redemptive leap will take place,[6] in the words of Engels, from the "realm of necessity" to the "realm of freedom." The worker has to be totally deprived of those attributes which make life tolerable; he has to be totally alienated from the products of his work, from his fellow man, from his true creative self ("Selbstentfremdung") and from nature. The bourgeoisie, as well as the proletariat, cannot escape an alienated condition. All this "has" to transpire in a the-worse-the-better process (i.e., more alienation under capitalism than under feudalism) "in order to arrive at faith in man."

For Marx, egoism and alienation are expressions of man's loss of community. Man is no longer a "species-being." Egoism flourishes without restraint under capitalism; there are no more limitations such as had existed under feudal society. It is necessary to transcend the civil society of capitalism—a Hobbesian-like state of nature[7]—in order to create a true community where egoism will no longer be possible. Such a transformation is not possible through mere political emancipation, which only entails replacing one set of exploiters with another, or by "good will." The first approach, political emancipation, is the erroneous strategy of Bruno Bauer;[8] the second, the moral appeal to the ruling classes to be "good" human beings, is the futile attitude of the Utopian Socialists, of the "True Socialists," and of other misguided "softs" such as Proudhon and Herzen. It is instructive that Marx detested Herzen and admired Chernyshevsky, a "hard." The latter approach, "good will," will accomplish nothing; it will only dull revolutionary consciousness. Lenin fully recognizes and steels himself against this danger. A flavor of Lenin's fanatical "hardness" is evident in his comment upon the enervating effect of music (such as that by Beethoven) in a famous conversation with Maxim Gorky.[9] Solzhenitsyn, in his perceptive psychological portrait of the Bolshevik leader, in the chapters published in book form as <u>Lenin in Zurich</u>, notes the debilitating impact of Inessa Armand upon Lenin. She causes him to doubt the worth of his self-dehumanization, his Rakhmetov-like pursuit of revolution; "she had shaken his certainties" in a manner which his wife and revolutionary helpmate, Krupskaya, never did.[10]

Escape from alienation can, for Marx, only come through class action by the real and not merely the existential proletariat. Like Marx, Solzhenitsyn recognizes that modern man has become excessively preoccupied with himself and is absorbed in self-love and his possessions. This narcissism is epitomized in Rusanov's obsession with his apartment in The Cancer Ward versus the very "unmodern" Matryona's indifference to her meager worldly goods. Solzhenitsyn believes that modern man's alienated, troubled condition can be overcome neither through material happiness nor through mere pragmatic success nor even through the more justifiable excellence of work. This is true even though work is an important therapy for Ivan Denisovich during the course of his famous "day."

According to Solzhenitsyn, man can transcend egoism as a form of alienation only by individual spiritual effort, by self-sacrifice, by helping others. By contrast, Marx denies the necessity of making an appeal to self-sacrifice,[11] although millions have sacrificed, and been sacrificed, on behalf of "scientific socialism." Models of self-sacrifice are evident in many of the characters in Solzhenitsyn's short stories and novels: in Matryona,[12] in Alyoshka the Baptist, who gently reminds Ivan Denisovich, and all of Solzhenitsyn's readers, that he is praying for the wrong things; in the individual bravery of the Tsarist officers, including such as Solzhenitsyn's own father, who died before Solzhenitsyn's birth, in East Prussia at the outset of World War I. Solzhenitsyn treats top Soviet military generals with contempt; they do not, in his estimation, transcend greed and self-serving qualities.[13] It is precisely the inability to overcome narrow self-concern which is the fatal flaw in the Soviet intelligentsia--the obrazovanshchina (those "with only an outward gloss"), as he pejoratively characterizes them in one of his essays in From Under the Rubble. The obrazovanshchina is an integral part of "modern man."

Solzhenitsyn affirms that a central aspect of overcoming egoism is the ability to love others. It is love which permits man to escape the prison of self--an internal prison from which Dostoevsky's "underground man," the archetype of modern man, cannot escape. Solzhenitsyn brilliantly portrays the lonely condition of Lenin in Zurich during the First World War and of Stalin in the Kremlin at the end of his life; neither is capable of love.[14] Strong men are not afraid to speak about love. Marx, ever

151

desirous to claim that his findings are "scientific," cannot find a place for love until man has reached full Communism.[15] Marx and Engels, in _The German Ideology_, ridicule Max Stirner for seeking a community of love before the bourgeoisie has been destroyed.[16] It is significant that Solzhenitsyn returns to the problem of love repeatedly in his writings. He discusses this problem extensively in his dialogues about Leo Tolstoy and the purpose of man's existence in _The Cancer Ward_ and in _August 1914_. Rusanov, the convincingly depicted Party apparatchik in _The Cancer Ward_, is totally alienated from the Soviet people whose "moral-political unity" he purports to represent; he violently attacks the Tolstoyan discussion of love as an "alien to Marxism-Leninism philosophy."[17] Rusanov has been nurtured upon a "class perspective," a philosophy of hatred of the "enemy," a tragically misplaced approach which Shulubin, the "ethical socialist," categorically dismisses in his conversation with Oleg Kostoglotov, the semi-autobiographical hero of _The Cancer Ward_. Shulubin's confession is an acknowledgment of moral transgression: his "silence" during the evils of the Stalin era. Andrei Sakharov and Svetlana Alliluyeva also call attention to Marxism's grounding itself upon hatred as a fundamental moral failing. Marx's hatred of the bourgeoisie was evident at least as early as 1844 (in his "Introduction" to his _Contribution to the Critique of Hegel's Philosophy of Right_).[18] Perceptive scholars have noted that this hatred of the bourgeoisie in Marx does not diminish but rather intensifies at the end of his life. Certainly, Lenin's entire mind-set is characterized by an intense hatred of the middle class, from which he himself derived. One can note Plekhanov's famous statement that Lenin turns his rear to the liberals while he, Plekhanov, turns his face to them. This quality of hatred, this need for an "enemy," is an integral part of Marxism-Leninism and is closely related to the official Soviet position maintained since Khrushchev's "open speech" to the Twentieth Party Congress in February 1956, that "peaceful coexistence" must _not_ extend to the realm of ideology. In other words, one must not cease to hate and be "vigilant" against the imperialists. Rejecting this Marxist demand to destroy the enemy, Solzhenitsyn insists that improvement in man's condition can only come through an inner transformation, through love, and not through hatred and destruction.

152

FREEDOM AND ITS LIMITS

Not only Marx but the West as a whole comes under Solzhenitsyn's critical eye on the question of freedom. A fundamental flaw in the Western concept of freedom is that it rests too heavily upon the pursuit of unlimited external freedom. Modern man has sought satisfaction where there can be none: in the ceaseless accumulation of material possessions. Give up your things and cherish only memory, is the advice of the former inmate of the camps.[19] In opposition to the misguided estimate of man's possibility for unbounded material prosperity Solzhenitsyn offers the idea of self-limitation and voluntary self-restraint.[20] Marx and Engels are somewhat ambiguous, in Part Two of The German Ideology, about the problem of man's "needs" and whether these needs will expand infinitely (shades of Condorcet?) under full Communism.[21] The moral crisis of the West, Solzhenitsyn believes, has evolved gradually since the beginning of secular humanism in the Renaissance and has accelerated since the Age of the Enlightenment. The orgy of self-gratification which Solzhenitsyn condemned so bluntly in his Harvard University June 1978 Commencement Address[22] has reached menacing proportions since 1945. The West has mistakenly believed that material prosperity can be accumulated without limit. Solzhenitsyn notes the warnings by the Club of Rome and others, and urges self-restraint.

Solzhenitsyn concludes that mankind's only recourse is to practice both personal and national self-restraint. In his Letter to the Soviet Leaders (1973/1974) he warns about disaster for the Russians and other peoples if Moscow does not turn inward. It must, he asserts, give up its attempts to support revolutions in the Southern Hemisphere, get out of the Mediterranean, remove itself from Eastern Europe and the Baltic States, and concentrate on the "Russian Northeast Space" (i.e., Siberia). Russia needs to recover from its warped and harrowing post-1917 experience; it needs time to recuperate and rejuvenate its spirit. It must concentrate upon internal, not external, concerns.[23] Russia's problems at home are all too numerous: alcoholism, the dire condition of agriculture, the shoddy quality of goods, etc. "The necessities for internal development are much more important for us /Russians_7," Solzhenitsyn advises Brezhnev and the other Soviet leaders, "as a nation, than the exigencies of the external spreading of our strength."[24]

153

National self-restraint must be matched by individual abnegation and voluntary self-limitation. Individuals and nations must cease striving for external accomplishments; they must turn inward and nurture their spiritual development. Solzhenitsyn praises genuine aristocracy for its sense of "self-control" (samoobladanie).[25] There is a certain similarity to this last observation by Solzhenitsyn in Marx's discussion of feudalism and alienation. Marx notes, in the "Paris Manuscripts," that the feudal lord does not seek to maximize profits, i.e., he does not treat his serfs as "commodities." In a similar vein, Solzhenitsyn, in a commentary on the famous 1968 Sakharov essay, notes that unchecked material progress such as Sakharov presupposes would be a literal "hell on earth."[26] Dostoevsky similarly condemns the naive optimism of the "Crystal-Palace" mentality in his elaboration of the objections of the "underground man" to unchecked modernity and rationalism. Solzhenitsyn and his associates such as the mathematician Shafarevich, who produced the collection of essays entitled From Under the Rubble, look upon the West with utter dismay. They believe that the West in the 1960's and 1970's represents the same moral nihilism, hedonism, and misplaced confidence in unlimited external freedom which misled Russia in the 1860's and 1870's and which, with a few exceptions such as the Vekhi group, dominated Russian thought up to the 1917 revolutions.[27] As recently as his BBC interview in February 1979 (on the fifth anniversary of his expulsion from the U. S. S. R.), Solzhenitsyn insistently warns that unchecked freedom in the West will only prepare the ground for those who will, without hesitation, impose "limits," just as the Bolsheviks did to bring an end to the chaos which ensued after the February (March) 1917 Revolution. This theme—the self-destructive nature of unchecked freedom and pluralism—is a core criticism of the West by Solzhenitsyn.[28] We may note that great political philosophers as widely separated in time as Plato, Machiavelli, and de Tocqueville, each in his own way, issue warnings similar to those of Solzhenitsyn. Those who cherish free institutions and seek to preserve them in times of general moral decline when, Machiavelli believes, a "Prince" will be necessary to curb excessive appetites, cannot lightly dismiss such warnings.

# FREEDOM, TRADITION, AND MODERN MAN

Both Marx and Solzhenitsyn concur that true freedom is possible only in community. While Marx and Solzhenitsyn are organic thinkers,[29] there is a fundamental difference. The founder of modern Communism looks forward to a community which can only exist beyond "pre-history."[30] Tradition is the chief force retarding the unfolding of genuine freedom for Marx. "The tradition of all the dead generations weighs like a nightmare /ein Alp/ on the brain of the living" is the renowned passage at the beginning of Marx's The Eighteenth Brumaire of Louis Bonaparte (1852).[31] Tradition, this "nightmare," must be destroyed, smashed by a "permanent revolution"..."until all more or less possessing classes have been forced out of their position of domination."[32] The prophetic vagueness of these words Stalin could invoke to justify his campaign to "eliminate the kulaks as a class." This fascination with "permanent revolution" has, in the words of Solzhenitsyn, driven "Jacobins early and late" to "cross over the threshold of evil." For Marx, only in a total revolution can man achieve true freedom and shed all of his traditional prejudices or false freedoms such as the opiate of religion, the desire for private property, and a yearning for the "idiocy of rural life." Only in a revolution can the proletariat "succeed in ridding itself of all the muck of ages and become fitted to found society anew."[33] It is in this sense that one can detect an existentialist theme in Marx: revolutionary existence must precede a genuine human existence. Promethean man must shatter the restraints of tradition and create himself. Man's freedom, for Marx, can be achieved only by negating both God and tradition.

For Solzhenitsyn, the Marxist attempt to destroy tradition is the essence of the wrong-headed arrogance of "scientific socialism." Solzhenitsyn, like Edmund Burke, is a conservative who believes that genuine freedom and community can flourish only on the basis of civility and tradition. Just as Burke violently attacks the attempt of the French Revolutionaries to shatter all organic ties with the French past, so Solzhenitsyn castigates the tabula-rasa mentality of the Bolsheviks who compulsively deny the worth of Old Russia. Solzhenitsyn believes that he has a mission to recapture the truth about twentieth-century Russia. To do this he seeks to undermine the central elements of Soviet mythology, the cult of Lenin and the sanctity of the

155

October Revolution, and to restore the memory of
what has been destroyed.  Accordingly, he has written the three-volume (seven-part) Gulag and has embarked upon the monumental task of producing a
series of creative works, the first of which is
August 1914, depicting Russia's travails in the
twentieth century.  From his neo-Slavophile perspective, the breaking of the vital threads of the Russian past started much earlier than in 1917.  Peter
the Great was the instigator of the rupture.[34]
Just as Burke is an advocate of slow, gradual, organic change, so is Solzhenitsyn.  One of the characters, clearly speaking for the author, at the end
of August 1914 states, "But if I do belong to it
/the Tsarist order/ , then I must enter into the
slow process of history /v terpelivyi protsess
istorii/, by work, by persuasion and gradual change
...."[35]  Solzhenitsyn does not deny that there were
ills in pre-1917 Russia.  He even admits in a moment of despair that "we /Russians/ are an Asian
people"[36] and that the cause of freedom advanced in
nineteenth-century Russia most when Russia was defeated in warfare.[37]  Nonetheless, he argues that
the Tsarist past was infinitely less oppressive and
stultifying than the Soviet present, that moral
freedom could grow under the authoritarian nature of
Old Russia in a way that has been impossible during
the totalitarian Soviet period.

"Die Arbeiter haben kein Vaterland" is the
ringing internationalist assertion of The Communist
Manifesto.  For Marx and Engels, nations and nationalism were increasingly irrelevant.[38]  Solzhenitsyn's attack on this Marxist denial of the validity
of nations is adamant.  It is a prime article of
faith of Solzhenitsyn and his circle which published
the essays From Under the Rubble.  Marx hated Russia; for him, it was the chief impediment to the
cause of revolution in Europe.[39]  For Solzhenitsyn,
the Russian nation is a very real and worthwhile
entity; it plays a vital moral role and nurtures the
traditions without which no individual can sustain
himself.  Solzhenitsyn is very much a "Russian patri-
ot,"[40] desirous of rescuing the best out of the Russian past and defending the pre-1917 Russian past
against the charge that it is responsible for the
moral evils of the Soviet regime.  Some critics of
Solzhenitsyn have suggested that he is, to a considerable degree, guilty of "Shatov's heresy" (i.e.,
a belief in Russia but not necessarily a belief in
God)--an aberration which Dostoevsky portrays with
great understanding in The Possessed.  It is

156

certainly true that both Dostoevsky and Solzhenitsyn are profoundly conscious of the Russian tradition and of the nature of the Russian community. But it is also true that both the creator of the "Legend of the Grand Inquisitor" and the exiled Solzhenitsyn deal with human concerns and problems which transcend limitations of time and national boundaries. Both Dostoevsky's "underground man" and his protagonist in The Possessed, Stavrogin (who ends his "superfluity" by suicide), are products of a desperate nineteenth-century Russian search for a new sense of Purpose (which Sinyavsky, under the pseudonym of "Abram Tertz," has probed so perceptively).[41] They also portray problems of "modern man" who has lost his traditional roots and is lonely and alienated. Similarly, Ivan Denisovich is a portrayal of the problems of survival among the camp inmates under Stalin. Simultaneously, Ivan Denisovich's experience illuminates general moral problems of human existence. It is hardly accurate to claim that Solzhenitsyn's appeal is limited only to Soviet or Russian audiences. He speaks to all who are attuned to the moral challenges and paradoxes of human existence, especially in our contemporary world.

INTERNAL AND EXTERNAL FREEDOM

Almost all of Solzhenitsyn's early works, those written before he began August 1914, reflect the searing impact of the Soviet camp system upon him: One Day in the Life of Ivan Denisovich; The First Circle; The Cancer Ward; and, above all, perhaps the greatest literary epic of the twentieth century, the three-volume Gulag. All of these writings deal, whether explicitly or implicitly, with the question of how an individual can maintain his integrity under the most harrowing of circumstances. Ivan Denisovich maintains considerable moral uprightness in the camps; the old man, "Iu-81," who is only very briefly but unforgettably described,[42] and Alyoshka, preserve perhaps even more of this vital substance of the soul. Fetiukov (to whom Solzhenitsyn, in the Gulag, compares the victim of the Great Purge, camp inmate, and World War II Soviet general, Aleksandr V. Gorbatov)[43] obviously lacks "a stable soul." Nerzhin, the semi-autobiographical protagonist in The First Circle, voluntarily leaves the relatively privileged sanctuary of the sharashka with its good food, adequate clothing, and most importantly, sufficient warmth. He accepts assignment to the camps

157

to escape participation in the Stalinist lie and to maintain his self-respect. Through his own free will that is an act of internal freedom, as the ancient Stoic philosophers correctly recognized,[44] he chooses the camps and all of the external suffering and risk that such a choice necessarily entails.[45]

Throughout his camp writings Solzhenitsyn is concerned with the paradoxical, yet profoundly vital problem of the relationship between man's external condition, which exerts a relative constraint upon his external freedom, and the maintenance of his inner integrity, his inner freedom.[46] Repeatedly, Solzhenitsyn poses the query: does one have more internal freedom inside or outside the Stalinist camps? Even though he has Nerzhin choose the camps over the _sharashka_, Solzhenitsyn frankly acknowledges, in the _Gulag_, that he, Solzhenitsyn, would not have survived to write about the camps unless he had spent some time in a Moscow _sharashka_.[47] Solzhenitsyn's concern for man's inner freedom is related to what Professor Richard Pipes of Harvard University has characterized as the "autonomous man" tradition in nineteenth and twentieth-century Russian thought. Its representatives would include figures such as Chaadaev, Khomyakov, Herzen (his essays _From the Other Shore_), Dostoevsky, Vladimir Solovyov, and the _Vekhi_ group (especially Berdyaev). In the recent Soviet period we should certainly wish to add to this list Pasternak (whose roots, to be sure, are in the "Silver Age" of pre-1917 Russia),[48] Sinyavsky and Solzhenitsyn--as well as the "Westerner" Amalrik, who asserts in his important dispute with Anatoli V. Kuznetsov the primacy of internal over external freedom.[49]

Solzhenitsyn's concern with man's inner life is integrally related to his Christian belief, which is not restricted to sympathy solely for Russian Orthodoxy: his admiration for the Catholic Church's role in Poland and for the Russian Baptists and for the Estonian Lutherans is quite evident from his writings. His religious commitment is not clearly discernible in his earlier works. In _One Day_ there is considerable empathy for Alyoshka the Baptist. But the protagonist, the peasant Ivan Denisovich Shukhov, is not apparently religious; in fact, at the end of this literary masterpiece Ivan Denisovich expresses contempt for the venal Russian Orthodox village priests. There are emerging hints of religious symbols in some of his subsequent major novels, such as _The First Circle_ and _The Cancer Ward_. But it is only with the _Gulag_, the publication of which was

158

precipitated by action taken by the K. G. B., that
Solzhenitsyn unequivocally spells out his Christian
conversion, which was a product of his camp experiences. He describes this self-discovery perhaps
most clearly in an important section of Volume Two
of his Gulag: Part IV, Chapter One, "The Ascent."
The title of this chapter does not refer to any
physical climb (such as passage out of the camps into the external "freedom" of Soviet society). Rather, he is revealing his own spiritual rebirth in
the camps and his recognition that the central concern of man must be his moral development, his relationship to God.[50] The key struggle always takes
place within each individual.[51] In one of his essays in From Under the Rubble Solzhenitsyn asks:

> External freedom in and of itself--can it be
> the goal of conscious living beings? Or is it
> only the form for the realization of other,
> higher aims? We are born already as creatures
> with internal freedom, freedom of the will,
> freedom of choice; the most important part of
> freedom is already given to us at birth. Ex-
> ternal, social freedom is very desirable for
> our undistorted development, but it is no more
> than a condition, a means; to consider it the
> goal of our existence is an absurdity /bes-
> smyslitsa_7. We can maintain our freedom firm-
> ly even in conditions of a lack of external
> freedom....[52]

Solzhenitsyn praises the Baptists such as Alyoshka in One Day for their spiritual equanimity in
the camps; they do indeed possess a very "stable
soul"; they realize that "externals" do not, in the
last analysis, constitute the key to a person's
life.[53] They put their trust in God and find in
that faith a moral strength to accept, and even wel-
come, physical deprivation, suffering, and even
death itself. It is perhaps the problem of death
which points up another central distinction between
Marx and Solzhenitsyn. If man is part of nature--
and nothing more, which is the position of Marx's
secular humanism--there can be no effective answer
to death, a final end to external man. Marx, in the
Economic and Philosophical Manuscripts, attempts to
provide some answer to this ultimate question and
can come up with no satisfactory solution other than
the brief comment that the question of God cannot be
asked and that the individual ends while the species
continues.[54] In a similar manner, the Party

159

apparatchik Rusanov in Solzhenitsyn's The Cancer Ward has no adequate answer, based as it is upon his mind-set of Marxism-Leninism, to the stark confrontation with the reality of death amidst the terminal cancer patients. For Solzhenitsyn, this lacuna in Marx and in his intellectual epigone Rusanov is also part of the "void" in modern man. Only in man's relationship to God, Solzhenitsyn concludes, can one find an acceptable answer to the inescapable fact of death--one's own as well as that of loved ones.

## CONCLUSION

Neither Marx nor Solzhenitsyn is a systematic political philosopher in the manner of a Thomas Hobbes, a thinker who exerted a profoundly negative impact upon Marx and whose philosophical nominalism certainly would please neither Marx nor Solzhenitsyn.[55] One can glean the occasional flashes of insight in their thought only by plowing through the vast terrain of their writings. Perhaps the key difference relevant to the present investigation between these two intellectual titans lies in the manner in which each thinker deals with the "cursed questions" (as Dostoevsky, Solzhenitsyn's spiritual progenitor, termed them) of human existence, such as death, courage, honor, power, freedom, political obligation, love, and hate. These problems Solzhenitsyn directly confronts; they are his prime concern. One may not necessarily agree with his treatment of the "big questions," but one cannot fault him for neglecting them. They loom out of all of his works, both long and short. Marx, even the "Young Marx" of 1843-1846, tends to avoid these issues. To him they are distractions and impediments to the prosecution of his declared war on the bourgeoisie.[56]

Solzhenitsyn's challenge to Marx is precisely on the moral level. Marx brushes aside moral questions as either irrelevant or hypocritical; only a "scientific approach" will demonstrate the "iron necessity" of proletarian revolution. Solzhenitsyn's answer to Marx is that modern man can escape his anxious and unsatisfying condition ("a condition of false freedom," as was suggested at the beginning of this essay) in which he is the captive of self-love and a morbid fixation upon material "things" only by moral self-restraint and self-sacrifice (see his "Lenten Letter to Pimen").[57] Only by developing his "inner self" and only as an individual moral personality can man achieve genuine satisfaction, "inner assurance"--a condition of the soul which is quite different from the illusory goal of "happiness." Solzhenitsyn's objection to Marxism-Leninism and to twentieth-century totalitarianism (he considers the two to be coterminous) is that they deny the autonomy of the free moral personality. He views authoritarianism such as Tsarist Russia and Franco's Spain as qualitatively different from totalitarianism. Authoritarianism has self-limits; it does not prevent moral development. Totalitarianism has no limits; it is "total"; it suffocates the human spirit.[58] Marxism-Leninism has stifled twentieth-century man. Marxism-Leninism has permitted modern man to "cross over the threshold of evil."[59] "Let Russia breathe," Solzhenitsyn implores. Public opinion existed in Tsarist Russia; it has been extinguished in the U. S. S. R.[60] Freedom for Marx, following Hegel but with the important proviso of the "Eleventh Thesis on Feuerbach," is action based upon the understanding and acceptance of historical necessity. Solzhenitsyn asserts that this seductive proposition purports to provide a way out for man. He argues that this approach, in fact, precludes a solution which can only be successfully grounded upon individual moral struggle--not upon acquiescence in the "inevitable."

Solzhenitsyn makes high moral demands on himself and others. He condemns the lack of epic courage in Krupskaya, Gorky,[61] Bukharin,[62] Yevtushenko, Shostakovich,[63] in himself (his own past lack of courage in the camps; that he himself could easily have become a "Bluecap" /a Chekist7 or a self-serving Soviet career officer)...as well as what he considers the pervasive "spirit of Munich" in the West.[64] "Live not according to the Lie!" is his stern categorical imperative to the Soviet obrazovanshchina...and to all of us. His moral exemplars are those who bear up nobly under adversity and maintain their integrity despite an unfavorable environment (e.g., "Iu-81" and Alyoshka in One Day, Matryona, Jan Palach). Throughout all of Solzhenitsyn's writings there is an uncompromising rejection of the environmentalist approach of Marxism (see Marx and Engels on "Fleur de Marie" in The Holy Family).[65] It is this false perspective, the Russian Nobel laureate contends, which has resulted in the ravages of the human spirit in the twentieth century.

Solzhenitsyn does not believe that he, or any other individual, has fully discovered or can fully grasp the Truth finally and without qualification

161

(see Kostoglotov's outburst at Rusanov in The Cancer Ward).[66] "No human being can know the future," he notes in the third volume of his Gulag. This hubris (that communism is "the resolution of the riddle of history," in the uniquely revealing language of the "Paris Manuscripts")[67] is one of Marxism's most profound errors. Solzhenitsyn, in the words of Sinyavsky-Tertz, is a "seeker," Marx is a "believer."[68] At this point we confront a deep moral paradox for Solzhenitsyn--and for ourselves, for we are not mere disinterested onlookers in this drama; we are not mere Mannheimian "free-floating intellectuals." While Solzhenitsyn rejects Marx's pretensions to absolute knowledge, he is also equally convinced that moral relativism contains no solution to the malaise of modern man. It is, in fact, moral relativism which has crippled the West and rendered it spiritually defenseless against the false pretensions of the "Progressive Doctrine." Solzhenitsyn believes that the only way to resolve this dilemma is through religious faith and repentance. It is never too late to make this choice. Good and evil run through the heart of each of us. Neither Marxist-Leninist socialism nor Western secular "happiness" (see Shulubin's warning to Oleg Kostoglotov, in The Cancer Ward, that "happiness" as a goal is only an "idol of the marketplace")[69] can fill the "void" in modern man. Only religious faith can accomplish that goal.

NOTES

1. See Karl Marx, Zur Judenfrage ("The Jewish Question": 1844), in Karl Marx and Friedrich Engels, Werke, Vol. I (East Berlin: Dietz Verlag, 1961), especially pp. 353-357 and 363-369; the quote is on p. 369. All subsequent footnote references to Marx and Engels in this essay will omit their first names and, where the reference is clear, their last names also. All subsequent footnote references in this essay to this multi-volume Werke ("Works") will omit the authors (Marx and Engels), the city (East Berlin), and the publisher (Dietz Verlag), but will include the volume number, the year of publication and the page number(s).

2. Marx, "Thesen über Feuerbach" ("Theses on Feuerbach"), in Werke, III (1959), pp. 5-6. One may legitimately ask of the author of this famous "Third Thesis on Feuerbach": how "rational" a solution is "revolutionizing praxis" (a solution set forth in the second paragraph of this "Third Thesis") to the dilemma (set forth in the first paragraph of this

162

same "Thesis") of how does one "educate the educa-
tor"?

3. Marx writes in the famous Economic and Philosophical Manuscripts of 1844, the so-called "Paris
Manuscripts" (Marx, Nationalökonomie und Philosophie, in Marx, Die Frühschriften /"The Early Writ-
ings7 , ed. by Siegfried Landshut /Stuttgart:  Alfred Kröner Verlag, 19537 , p. 265) that there "wird
in der Wirklichkeit einen sehr rauhen und weitläufi-
gen Prozess durchmachen."

4. See the important polemic between David Resnick and Shlomo Avineri on the relationship in the
thought of Marx between "crude communism" and the
"dictatorship of the proletariat":  "Crude Communism
and Revolution," The American Political Science Review 70, no. 4 (December 1976), pp. 1136-1155.  I
find that the argument of Avineri (stressing considerable congruence between the concepts of "crude communism" and the "dictatorship of the proletariat")
is more convincing than the excessively convoluted
position of Resnick.

5. Aleksandr Solzhenitsyn, "Raskaianie i samoogranichenie kak kategorii natsional'noi zhini" ("Repentance and Self-Restraint as Categories of National Life"), in Agursky, M.S. et al., Iz-pod glyb.
Sbornik Statei Moskva, 1974 /"From Under the Rubble.
A Collection of Articles.  Moscow, 1974"/ (Paris:
YMCA Press, 1974), p. 117.  This work will be subsequently cited as Iz-pod glyb.  All subsequent footnote references in this essay to Solzhenitsyn's
works will omit his first name and, where the reference is clear, his last name also.

6. About as close as Marx ever comes to acknowledging, openly, the redemptive role of the proletariat is in his "Zur Kritik der Hegelschen Rechtsphilosophie.  Einleitung" ("Contribution to the Critique of Hegel's Philosophy of Right:  Introduction"), in Werke, I (1961), p. 390.  There he speaks
of "die völlige Wiedergewinnung /regeneration7 des
Menschen."  Despite the lack of explicit discussion,
the assumption of a redemptive role for the proletariat (i.e., mankind) is central to the thought of
Marx and Engels.  The present essay does not attempt
to evaluate the fascinating controversy over the relationship between Marx and Engels and the relative
contributions of each to the thought of "scientific
socialism."

7. My late father, William Yandell Elliott, has
exerted and continues to exert profound intellectual
and moral influence upon my life and thought.  He
once wrote (in his Western Political Heritage /N. Y.:

163

Prentice-Hall, 1949/ , p. 704; he is quoting his old tutor, A. D. Lindsay of Balliol College, in the latter's The Modern Democratic State /N. Y.: Oxford University Press, 1947/ , p. 83) that Marx called Hobbes the "father of us all." While I have never found such a direct statement by Marx, this generalization is basically accurate, both in a positive sense (Marx admired Hobbes' materialism and rejection of theism) and in a negative sense. Concerning the negative impact of Hobbes, Marx and Engels wrote (Die heilige Familie oder Kritik der kritischen Kritik. Gegen Bruno Bauer and Konsorten /"The Holy Family or Critique of Critical Criticism. Against Bruno Bauer and Associates": 1845/ , in Werke, II /1959/ , p. 136) that "Materialism /with Hobbes/ became hostile to humanity." The "Ninth and Tenth Theses on Feuerbach" are certainly references to Hobbes as a representative of the "old materialist" school--which Marx believes must be transcended by the organic perspective of a "socialized humanity." See also Marx's utilization of Hobbes' phrase, bellum omnium contra omnes ("the war of all against all"), to characterize the anarchical condition of bourgeois "civil society" (Zur Judenfrage, in Werke, I /1961/ , p. 356). For further references by Marx and Engels on Hobbes, see their Die deutsche Ideologie ("The German Ideology": 1846) in Werke, III (1959), pp. 311, 396, and 397.

8. See Marx, Zur Judenfrage, in Werke, I (1961), pp. 347-377.

9. Lenin told Maxim Gorky (quoted in Georg Lukács, Lenin. A Study on the Unity of His Thought /Cambridge, Mass.: M. I. T. Press, 1971/ , p. 94), "'The Appassionata is the most beautiful thing I know; I could listen to it every day. What wonderful, almost superhuman music! I always think with pride--perhaps it is naive of me--what marvelous things human beings can do.' Then he screwed up his eyes, smiled, and added regretfully, 'But I can't listen to music too often. It works on my nerves so that I would rather talk foolishness and stroke the heads of people who live in this filthy hell and can still create such beauty. But now is not the time to stroke heads--you might get your hand bitten off. We must hit people mercilessly on the head, even when we are ideally against any violence between men. Oh! our work is hellishly difficult.'"

10. Solzhenitsyn, Lenin v Tsiurikhe. Glavy /"Lenin in Zurich. Chapters"/ (Paris: YMCA Press, 1975), pp. 66, 68, 71.

164

11. See Marx and Engels, Die deutsche Ideologie, in Werke, III (1959), p. 229.

12. See Solzhenitsyn, "Matrenin dvor" /"Matryona's Household"/ , in id., Rasskazy /"Stories"/ (Frankfurt/Main: Possev-Verlag, 1976), pp. 215-259, especially the famous concluding epitaph for Matryona (on p. 259).

13. Solzhenitsyn, ARKHIPELAG GULag 1918-1956. Opyt khudozhestvennogo issledovaniia /"The Gulag Archipelago 1918-1956. An Expermient in Literary Imagination"/ , III (Paris: YMCA-Press, 1975), p. 35. All subsequent footnote references to this three-volume Russian language edition (Vol. I, 1973= Parts I & II; Vol. II, 1974 = Parts III & IV; Vol. III, 1975 = Parts V, VI & VII) will omit the author's name, the city of publication, and the publisher and the year of publication; references will be as follows: GULag, volume number and page number(s).

14. Lenin v Tsiurikhe, p. 89, and Solzhenitsyn, V kruge pervom /"The First Circle"/ (Frankfurt/Main: Possev-Verlag, 1969; Vol. III of Solzhenitsyn's six-volume Sobranie Sochinenii /"Collected Works"/ ), p. 164.

15. See the brief but moving passage on love in the unpublished "Paris Manuscripts" at the end of the section of "Money" (Die Frühschriften, p. 301). Marx sternly repressed this aspect of his thought-- the importance of love, just as Lenin did (e.g., in his previously-noted relationship with Inessa Armand and his fear that listening to Beethoven's music would make him "soft"--see above, ft. #9). The consequences for mankind have been disastrous.

16. Die deutsche Ideologie, in Werke, III (1959), pp. 191-192.

17. Rusanov states (Rakovyi korpus /"The Cancer Ward"/ /Frankfurt/Main: Possev-Verlag, 1969/ , p. 123) that "...chto moral' /of love/ ne nasha."

18. "Zur Kritik der Hegelschen Rechtsphilosophie. Einleitung," in Werke, I (1961), p. 388.

19. GULag, I, pp. 512, 541.

20. Solzhenitsyn notes ("Raskaianie i samoogranichenie," in Iz-pod glyb, p. 144), "After the Western ideal of unlimited freedom, after the Marxist understanding of necessity--here is the true Christian definition of freedom. Freedom is self-restriction! Restriction of the self for the sake of others!" Emphasis in the original.

21. Marx and Engels do suggest, in Die deutsche Ideologie, in two very interesting footnotes (see Werke, III /1959/ , pp. 238-239 ft. and

246 ft.) that man's needs will expand infinitely and so will his ability to satisfy these wants. But, both of these footnotes are crossed out in the original, unpublished manuscript. (Die deutsche Ideologie was written in 1845-1846 but was first published in complete form only in 1932 in the MEGA.) The Soviet-East German edition of the Werke of Marx and Engels, in a model of careful scholarship, preserves these two footnotes as Marx and Engels originally conceived them.

22. I was fortunate enough to have been present in the Tercentenary Theater in the Harvard Yard when Solzhenitsyn delivered this important speech. See Solzhenitsyn, "The Exhausted West," HARVARD Magazine 80, No. 6 (July-August 1978), pp. 21-25. "Destructive and irresponsible freedom has been granted boundless space" (p. 22) is a representative sample of this strong polemic.

23. See Solzhenistyn, Pis'mo Vozhdiam Sovetskogo Soiuza /"Letter to the Soviet Leaders"/ (Paris: YMCA-Press, 1974), Chapters 4 and 5.

24. Ibid., p. 35; emphasis in the original.

25. GULag, II, p. 43.

26. "Na vozvrate dykhaniia i soznaniia (Po povodu traktata A. D. Sakharova "Razmyshleniia o progresse, mirnom sosushchestvovanii i intellektual'noi svobode')" /"On the Return of Breathing and Consciousness (On the Treatise of A. D. Sakharov 'Reflections on Progress, Peaceful Coexistence and Intellectual Freedom')" /, in Iz-pod glyb, p. 19.

27. See Solzhenitsyn's chapter, the "Obrazovanshchina," in ibid., pp. 217-259.

28. See Solzhenitsyn, "The Exhausted West" (cited above, ft. #22).

29. Marx and Engels do note, obliquely (Die deutsche Ideologie, in Werke, III /1959 /, p. 145), Aristotle's dictum that man is a zoon politikon. Some would perhaps ask: why did Marx, who knew his Aristotle quite well and specifically acknowledges Aristotle's characterization of man as a zoon politikon, believe that the state (and, therefore, "politics") could "wither away" (actually Engels' phrase--see above, ft. #6)? In defense of Marx one should acknowledge that "politics" in the Greek polis (even in Aristotle's time when there was already beginning a transition to the Hellenistic world of empire) meant an intensely rich communal life, which encompassed far more than political activity did in nineteenth-century Europe. On this general point see the very scholarly "Editor's Introduction" by Joseph O'Malley to Karl Marx, Critique of Hegel's "Philosophy of Right" (London: Cambridge University Press, 1970), especially pp. xvii and xl-1.

30. Marx, Zur Kritik der Politischen Ökonomie: Vorwort ("Preface to A Contribution to the Critique of Political Economy"), in Werke, XIII (1961), p. 9.

31. Die achtzehnte Brumaire des Louis Bonaparte, in Werke, VIII (1960), p. 115.

32. Marx and Engels, Ansprache des Zentralbehörde an den Bund vom März 1850 ("Address of the Central Authority to the /Communist/ League: March 1850"), in Werke, VII (1960), p. 248.

33. Marx and Engels wrote (Die deutsche Ideologie, in Werke, III /1959 /, p. 70), "...sich den genzen alten Dreck vom Halse zu schaffen und zu einer neuen Begründung der Gesellschaft befähigt zu werden."

34. At times Solzhenitsyn admits (e.g., GULag, II, p. 296) that things were wrong in Russia even before ("da poran'she") Peter the Great.

35. Avgust Chetyrnadtsatogo /"August 1914"/ (Paris: YMCA-Press, 1971), p. 537.

36. GULag, I, p. 152: "My narod aziatskii...." The influence of Karl A. Wittfogel (and the theory of the "Asiatic mode of production" and "Oriental despotism") upon Solzhenitsyn's group is clearly evident in Iz-pod glyb. See especially the first essay by Shafarevich ("Sotsializm," pp. 29-72) and also Melik Agurskii, "Sovremennye obshchestvenno-ekonomicheskie sistemy i ikh perspektivy" ("Contemporary Socioeconomic Systems and Their Prospects"), in ibid., p. 81. See also GULag, II, pp. 84, 91, 151 ("Uzhe sem' stoletii znaia aziatskoe rabstvo, Rossiia...."), 152, 442, 502-503, 522 ("...tianut egipetskie murav'i parovozy na sneg...."). Whether Solzhenitsyn realizes it or not, the utilization of Wittfogel's theories is not entirely compatible with a neo-Slavophile interpretation of Russian history. Perhaps Solzhenitsyn's sensitivity to Russia's semi-Asiatic past should caution us not to seek to reduce his thought to a narrow mold.

37. GULag, I, p. 277; and Avgust Chetyrnadtsatogo, p. 137.

38. For a somewhat different view of Marx and Engels on nationalism from that held by the present author see the classic study by Solomon F. Bloom, The World of Nations. A Study of the National Implications in the Work of Karl Marx (N. Y.: Columbia University Press, 1941).

39. See Marx and Engels, The Russian Menace to Europe. A Collection of Articles, Speeches, Letters and News Dispatches. Selected and Edited by Paul W. Blackstock and Bert F. Hoselitz (Glencoe, Ill,: The Free Press, 1952).

40. See the perceptive study by Carl A. Linden, Soviet Politics and the Revival of Russian Patriotism. Soviet Rulers, Dissident Patriots and Solzhenitsyn (Institute for Sino-Soviet Studies, The George Washington University, 1976, 76 pp.). I should like to acknowledge my enormous intellectual debt (past, present, and future) to my very good friend and colleague, Carl A. Linden. Naturally, he is not responsible for any errors of fact or of judgment in the present article. For a hostile view of Solzhenitsyn as a Russian nationalist extremist, see Olga Carlisle (the granddaughter of Leonid Andreev, the early twentieth-century Russian writer), "Reviving Myths of Holy Russia," The New York Times Magazine, September 16, 1979, pp. 50, 57, 60, 64, 65, and 66. See also the same viewpoint in Olga Carlisle's "Solzhenitsyn and Russian Nationalism. An Interview with Andrei Sinyavsky," The New York Review of Books, Vol. 26, No. 18 (November 22, 1979), pp. 3-6. The growing disenchantment of Olga Carlisle with Solzhenitsyn is evident in her book, Solzhenitsyn and the Secret Circle (N. Y.: Holt, Rinehart & Winston, 1978). Carlisle and, to a lesser extent, Sinyavsky tend to blur the distinction between the perspective of Solzhenitsyn and the views of the anti-Semitic lunatic fringe of the Russian dissidents. (A sample of the latter may be seen in the recent Russian-language, 18-page samizdat polemic, dated Moscow, February 23, 1979: OBRASHCHENIE RUSSKOGO OSVOBODITEL'NOGO DVIZHENIIA (ROD) K RUSSKOMU I UKRAINSKOMU NARODAM" /"ADDRESS OF THE RUSSIAN EMANCIPATION MOVEMENT (ROD) TO THE RUSSIAN AND UKRAINIAN PEOPLES"/.) Professor Linden and the present author would sharply distinguish between Solzhenitsyn's Russian patriotism and the attitude of the extremist fringe of the Russian nationalists. Harrison E. Salisbury of The New York Times has also argued for making such a distinction ("A strong line must be drawn..."); see his article, "Stalin Makes A Comeback," The New York Times Magazine, December 23, 1979, p. 30. Whether such a distinction is correct may be of considerable significance in the post-Brezhnev struggle for the Russians' ideational loyalties.

41. Abram Tertz (Andrei Sinyavsky), On Socialist Realism, Introduction by Czeslaw Milosz, (N. Y.: Pantheon-Random, 1960), pp. 23-95.

42. See Solzhenitsyn, Odin den' Ivana Denisovicha ("One Day of Ivan Denisovich"), in Rasskazy, pp. 121-122.

43. "But the general /Gorbatov/ behaved not like /Ivan Denisovich_/Shukhov, but like Fetiukov"; GULag, II, p. 331.

44. There is a favorable reference to the Stoics in GULag, I, p. 512.

45. V kruge pervom, pp. 803-804.

46. See, inter alia, GULag, II, pp. 330, 594-595, 617-618; and, GULag, III, pp. 95-96, 113, 433.

47. Solzhenitsyn notes (GULag, II, p. 476) that "A fortuitous circumstance /pobochnoe obstoiatel'-stvo/ saved me /in the Archipelago/ --mathematics."

48. An interesting problem is why Solzhenitsyn has not commented on Pasternak's Dr. Zhivago. There is a single favorable reference to Pasternak in each of the three volumes of the GULag, two to Pasternak's poem, "Lieutenant Schmidt" (GULag, I, p. 605, and GULag, II, p. 183), and one to the harassment of Pasternak in 1959 shortly before his death (GULag, III, p. 480). Certainly, Solzhenitsyn must have read Dr. Zhivago, a novel which embodies many ideas close to those of Solzhenitsyn: Christian self-sacrifice, love for Russia, the lack of moral integrity and inner freedom among Marxist revolutionaries, etc. Solzhenitsyn spent time in the Stalinist camps, Pasternak did not. But, Solzhenitsyn neither admires all those who "sat" in Stalinist camps nor despises all those who did not. Solzhenitsyn, in 1970, benefitted from reflecting upon Pasternak's sad experience with the Nobel Prize for literature award in 1958. Solzhenitsyn, who has commented extensively and penetratingly on a wide range of Russian authors (both pre- and post-1917) such as Dostoevsky, Tolstoy, Chekhov, Gorky, Sholokhov, and others, is strangely silent on Dr. Zhivago. Does Solzhenitsyn believe that Iurii Zhivago represents a false epic? I have discussed this puzzle with the late Max Hayward; he had no ready solution to this problem.

49. See Andrei Amalrik, "An Open Letter to Kuznetsov," SURVEY, no. 74-75 (Winter-Spring 1970), pp. 95-102. In this "open letter" Amalrik reproaches Kuznetsov: "You speak all the time of freedom, but of external freedom, the freedom around us, and you say nothing of inner freedom, that is, the freedom according to which the authorities can do much to a man but by which they are powerless to deprive him of his moral values."

50. See GULag, II, Part IV, Chap. 1 "Voskhozhdenie," especially pp. 594-604.

51. Ibid., p. 603.

52. "Na vozvrate dykhaniia i soznaniia," Iz-pod glyb, pp. 24-25; emphasis in the original.

169

53. GULag, III, pp. 114-117.
54. Marx writes (Die Frühschriften, p. 239), "Der Tod scheint als ein harter Sieg der Gattung über das Individuum und ihrer Einheit zu widersprechen; aber das bestimmte Individuum ist nur ein bestimmtes Gattungswesen, als solches sterblich."
55. For the comments by Marx and Engels on Bacon and Hobbes and nominalism and materialism see Die heilige Familie, in Werke, II, pp. 135-136.
56. See Isaiah Berlin, Karl Marx. His Life and Environment, 2nd ed. (London: Oxford University Press, 1956), pp. 8-9.
57. See A Lenten Letter to Pimen, Patriarch of All Russia. Trans. by Keith Armes; commentary by Wassilij Alexeev; edited by Theofanis G. Stavrou (Minneapolis, Minn.: Burgess Publishing Co., 1972), pp. 5-8.
58. See GULag, III, pp. 84-105.
59. GULag, I, pp. 181-182.
60. See above, ft. #58.
61. Solzhenitsyn attacks Maxim Gorky strongly in all three volumes of the GULag, especially volumes I and II. For a sample of this bitter condemnation, see GULag, II, pp. 78-85 and, especially,93.
62. Solzhenitsyn's contempt for Bukharin (who lacked "an individual point of view") is evident in GULag, I, pp. 111 ft #8, 140 ft. #27, 197, 406-419. For a quite different, sympathetic appraisal of Bukharin, see Stephen F. Cohen, Bukharin and the Bolshevik Revolution. A Political Biography 1888-1938 (N. Y.: Alfred Knopf, 1974).
63. For Solzhenitsyn's attack on Shostakovich, see GULag, II, pp. 119 ft. #46, 415, and GULag, III, p. 54 ft. #4. For a cogent analysis of one of the reasons for Solzhenitsyn's rejection of Shostakovich see Solomon Volkov, "Introduction," in Testimony. The Memoirs of Dmitri Shostakovich, as related to and edited by Solomon Volkov; translated from the Russian by Antonina W. Bouis (N. Y.: Harper & Row, 1979), p. xli and p. xli ft. As Volkov correctly notes, Solzhenitsyn cannot accept Shostakovich's secular perspective that "Death is all-powerful" (the words of Shostakovich's Fourteenth Symphony /1969_7) and "There is no afterlife" (ibid., p. 243). See also ibid., pp. xl, 186-187, 195, 242, 243, 270, for more comments by Shostakovich on Solzhenitsyn as a self-righteous "luminary" and (along with Stalin) a "sick person." The theme of the fear of the finality of death pervades Shostakovich's "Memoirs" (which I assume to be genuine, particularly

on <u>this</u> point). This fascinating, gloomy near-auto-
biography holds out little hope ("my life...was gray
and dull," Shostakovich concludes at the end of his
account; ibid., p. 275).

     64. "Nobelevskaia lektsiia 1970 goda po litera-
ture" ("The 1970 Nobel Literature /Award/ Speech"),
in <u>Sobranie sochinenii</u> Vol. VI, 2nd ed., enlarged
and revised (Frankfurt/Main: Possev-Verlag, 1973),
pp. 362-363.

     65. <u>Die heilige Familie</u>, in <u>Werke</u>, II (1959),
pp. 178-187.

     66. <u>Rakovyi korpus</u>, p. 157.

     67. Marx writes (<u>Die Frühschriften</u>, p. 235),
"Er ist das aufgelöste Rätsel der Geschichte und
weiss sich als diese Lösung."

     68. Tertz (Sinyavsky), pp. 30-37 and 58-59.

     69. <u>Rakovyi korpus</u>, p. 491

# The Contributors

CHARLES F. ELLIOTT is Associate Professor of Political Science and International Affairs at George Washington University, Washington, D. C.

CARL A. LINDEN is Associate Professor of Political Science and International Affairs at George Washington University, Washington, D. C.

EUSEBIO M. MUJAL-LEÓN is Assistant Professor of Government at Georgetown University, Washington, D. C.

PAUL E. SIGMUND is Professor of Politics at Princeton University, Princeton, New Jersey.

MICHAEL J. SODARO is Assistant Professor of Political Science and International Affairs at George Washington University, Washington, D. C.

JOAN BARTH URBAN is Professor of Political Science at Catholic University, Washington, D. C.

SHARON L. WOLCHIK is Assistant Professor of Political Science and International Affairs at George Washington University, Washington, D. C.

# Index

Acción Democratica, 22
AFTC, 86
Alienation, 150
Allende, Salvador, 2, 5, 6, 11, 24, 25, 27, 29, 32, 38, 88
Alliluyeva, Svetlana, 152
Althusser, 124
Amalrik, Andrei, 158, 169
American founders, 18
APRA, 22
Arbenz, Jacobo, 23
Argentina, 20, 25
Aristotle, 166
Armand, Inessa, 150
Aron, Raymond, 123
August 1914, 152, 156, 157
Auschwitz, 124
Austro-Marxist School, 91
Avineri, Shlomo, 163
Azcárate, Manuel, 95, 99

Ballesteros, Jaime, 97
Baptists, Russian, 158, 159
Batista, 26
Bauer, Bruno, 150
Bauer, Otto, 69
Beethoven, Ludwig van, 150, 164
Benoist, Jean-Marie, 123, 125, 138, 139, 143, 144
Berdyaev, 158

Berlin Conference of European Communist Parties, 1976, 47
Berlinguer, Enrico, 39, 44, 48, 50, 52, 53, 54, 62
Bernstein, Eduard, 12, 37, 92
Bobbio, Norberto, 78
Boffa, Giuseppe, 64
Bolivia, 23, 25
Brazil, 23, 24, 27, 33
Brezhnev, Leonid, 9, 48, 55, 153
Bukharin, Nikolai, 70, 81, 161, 170

Cancer Ward, 151, 152, 157, 158, 160, 162, 165
Cardenas, Lazaro, 22, 26
Carlisle, Olga, 168
Carrillo, Santiago, 7, 39, 45, 46, 48, 50, 51, 52, 53, 84, 86, 88, 89, 90, 92, 93, 94, 95, 96, 97, 98, 99, 100, 101
Castro, Fidel, 23, 25, 26, 30, 31, 88
Catholicism, 27, 67
Catholics, 45, 47
Ceausescu, 56
Chaadaev, Peter, 158
Chernyshevsky, 150
Chile, 2, 11, 20, 21, 22, 23, 24, 25, 26, 38, 44, 88
China, People's Republic of, 43, 49, 134, 135, 136
Christian Democrats, Italian, 43, 44

173

Christianity, 158, 159
Churchill, Winston, 18
CIA, 25
Civic culture, 16, 17, 19
Civil order, 9, 10, 14,
   15, 16
Civil War in France, 130
Claudín, Fernando, 88, 89,
   94
Cohn-Bendit, Daniel, 128
   129
Cold War, 23
Colombia, 24
Comintern, 20, 48, 49
Comisiones obreras, 98
   99
Communist Manifesto, 130,
   156
Compromesso storico,43-4
Contribution to the crit-
   ique of Hegel's Philo-
   sophy of Right, 152,
   163
CPSU, 38, 43, 44, 45, 47,
   48, 49, 50, 52, 53
Craxi, Bettino, 57, 61
Critica Marxista, 63
"Crude communism," 149
Cuba, 20, 22, 26, 29, 30
Cunhal, Alvaro, 7, 46
Czechoslovakia, 24, 43,
   45, 46, 48, 55, 56, 61,
   100
Czechoslovakia, Communist
   Party of, 8

Dahl, Robert, 16
Daniel, Yulii, 100
Debray, Regis, 29, 30
Democracy, 10, 11, 14, 18
Democratic centralism,
   11, 17, 68, 69
Dependencia, 31
Derrida, Jacques, 125
Despotism, 5, 19
Destalinization, 42
Dictatorship of the pro-
   letariat, 32, 149
Doctor Zhivago, 169
Dollé, Jean Paul, 137,
   138, 142, 143, 148

Dostoyevsky, Fyodor, 151,
   154, 156, 157, 158, 160
Dubcek, Alexander, 56

Early Writings (Marx),
   170, 171
Eastern Europe, 36, 42,
   47, 52, 55, 56, 60, 63
   64, 66, 68, 71, 74, 95
Economic and Philosophical
   Manuscripts ("Paris
   Manuscripts"), 154, 159
   162, 163, 165
Ecuador, 33
Egoism, 150
Eighteenth Brumaire of
   Louis Bonaparte, 155
Elliott, William, 163
Embourgeoisement, 86
Engels, Friedrich, 24, 30,
   39, 152, 153, 156, 161,
   166, 167
Eurocommunism, 1-19, 36-
   59, 138
European Parliament, 47,
   55
Espresso, 61
Europe, Eastern
   SEE Eastern Europe

Fichte, Johann, 132, 139
Fifth Republic, 128
First Circle, 157, 158
Foucault, Michel, 124, 125
France, 5, 6, 13, 14
France, Communist Party of
   SEE PCF
Franco, Francisco, 45, 49,
   86, 88, 98, 102
Freedom, 10, 150
Frente Popular, 22
From Under the Rubble,
   151, 154, 156, 159, 163,
   165, 167

Gallego, Ignacio, 97, 99
Gaullism, 123, 129
German Ideology, The, 152,
   153, 165, 166, 167
German SPD, 47
Germany, 2

174

Glucksman, André, 125, 131, 132, 133, 137, 138, 139, 140, 144, 146
Gorbatov, Aleksandr, 157
Gorky, Maxim, 150, 161, 170
Gramsci, 70, 74, 81, 90, 96
Gruppi, Luciano, 63, 65, 66, 72, 81
Guatemala, 23
Guevara, Che, 29, 30
Gulag Arkhipelago, 13, 156, 157, 158, 159, 162, 167

Havana, 23
Haya de la Torre, 21, 22
Hegel, Georg, 132, 139, 140
Helsinki Agreement, 143
Herzen, Alexander, 150, 158
Hilferding, Rudolf, 91
Hobbes, Thomas, 150, 160, 163-64
Holy Family, 161
Hoxha, Enver, 56
Huelga nacional, 86, 88, 110
Human rights, 10, 15
Hungary, 42, 54, 55

Ibárruri, Dolores, 99
Idea of progress, 4
Ideology, 2
Italy, 2, 5, 6, 8, 14, 16, 60-83
Italy, Communist Party of SEE PCI

Jacobins, 155
Jambet, Christian, 134, 137, 143, 144
Japan, 138
Jewish Question, 162, 164
Judeo-Christian tradition, 19
Jünger, Ernst, 140

Kautsky, Karl, 92
KGB, 107
Khrushchev, Nikita, 9, 38, 42, 152

Krupskaya, Nadezhda, 150, 151, 161
Kuznetsov, 158, 169

Labriola, 70
Lacan, Jacques, 124, 125
Lardreau, Guy, 134, 135, 136, 137, 143, 147
Latifundia, 21
Lenin, 2, 9, 12, 26, 30, 38, 39, 60, 62, 63, 64, 65, 67, 81, 132, 135, 136, 138, 150, 152, 155
Lenin in Zurich, 150, 151, 164
Leninism, 1, 6, 7, 8, 10, 12, 17, 50, 60-83, 85, 86, 88, 90, 94, 95, 96, 97, 100, 102
Leninists, 124
"Lenten Letter to Pimen" 160
Letter to the Soviet Leaders, 153
Levi-Strauss, Claude, 125
Lévy, Bernard-Henri, 124, 133, 137, 138, 139, 140, 141, 142, 143, 144
Lévy, Françoise, 133, 134, 136
Lincoln, Abraham, 16
Lin Piao, 136
Lister, Enrique, 94
Longo, Luigi, 44
Love, 151-52

Machiavelli, 6, 154
Maoism, Maoists, 124, 129, 130, 134, 135, 136
Mao Tse-tung, 3, 88, 134, 135, 136, 137, 142, 145, 147
Marchais, George, 48, 139, 143
Mariategui, Juan Carlos, 21
Marx, Karl, 1, 3, 4, 5,

175

10, 13, 38, 39, 149-71
Marxism, 1-19, 47, 85, 87, 90, 97
Marxism-Leninism, 41, 43, 67, 77
Matryona's Home, 151, 161, 165
Mexico, 21, 22, 33
MIR, 23, 25
Mitterand, François, 46
Mollet, Guy, 3
Moro, Aldo, 79

Nagy, Imre, 56
NATO, 38, 44
Natta, Alessandro, 81
Nemo, Philippe, 125, 143, 148
"New Philosophers" (France), 123, 148
Nicaragua, 26
Nietzsche, Friedrich, 132, 139, 140
Nihilism, 15

Obrazovanshchina, 151, 161
October Revolution, 39, 48, 49, 50, 53, 63, 100
OLAS, 24
One Day in the Life of Ivan Denisovich, 151, 157, 158, 161
Organización Sindical, 98
Ortodoxo Party, 23
Ouvrièriste, 51

Palach, Jan, 161
Pasternak, Boris, 158, 169
Paris Commune, 132
PCE, 36-59, 84-122
PCF, 36-59, 93, 95, 124, 129, 135, 137, 138, 145
PCI, 36-59, 60-83, 85, 92, 95
"Permanent Revolution," 149
Perón, Isabel, 25
Perón, Juan, 22
Peru, 21, 22, 23, 24, 26
Peter the Great, 167
Pipes, Richard, 158

Plato, 4, 138, 142, 154
Plekhanov, 152
Pluralism, 14, 15, 17, 18
Poland, 53, 54, 55
"Polyarchy," 16
Polycentrism, 36, 40-47
Popular Front, 22, 97, 102
Portugal, 7
Portugal, Communist Party of, 38, 46, 55, 93, 102
Possessed, The, 156, 157
Prebisch, Raul, 27
Procacci, Giulio, 67, 80-81
Proudhon, 144, 145, 150

Radical Party, 22
Radio España Independiente, 102
Rakhmetov, 150
Regime, theory of stages, 4-5
Relativism, 15, 19
Resnick, David, 163
Revisionism, 36, 37
Revolution, 3
Rinascita, 69, 71, 72, 76
Roy, M. N., 21
Russian Orthodoxy, 158

Sacristán, Manuel, 94
Sakharov, Andrei, 152, 154
Sánchez Móntero, Simon, 99
Sartorius, Nicolás, 97, 98
Sartre, Jean-Paul, 144
Scandinavia, 41
Scarponi, Alberto, 69
Self-control (samoobladanie), 154
Semprún, Jorge, 89
Shostakovich, Dmitri, 161, 170
Siberia, 153
Sinyavsky, Andrei, 100, 157, 158, 162, 168

176

Soares, Mario, 46
Solipsism, 16
Solovyov, Vladimir, 158
Solzhenitsyn, 13, 100, 101,
   124, 137, 145, 147, 149-
   71
Soviet dissidents, 13
Soviet Union, 8, 10, 26,
   36, 42, 43, 45, 46, 47,
   49, 50, 52, 53, 60, 61,
   66, 68, 71, 74, 79, 85,
   95, 99, 100
Soviet Union, Communist
   Party of,
   SEE CPSU
Spain, 5, 6, 8
Spain, Communist Party of,
   SEE PCE
Spanish Civil War, 85, 102
Stabilization Plan, 91
Stalin, 7, 9, 47, 49, 50,
   51, 64, 85, 96, 136, 137,
   138, 141, 145, 147, 151
Stirner, Max, 152
Suárez, Adolfo, 86
Sunkel, Osvaldo, 31

Terrorism, 13, 14
Theses on Feuerbach, 161,
   162, 164
"Third Way" (La Terza Via),
   53, 61, 71, 72, 73, 74,
   75, 76, 77, 78
Third World, 2
Tito, 41, 47, 49, 56
Tocqueville, 18, 154
Togliatti, Palmiro, 40, 42,
   43, 45, 47, 49, 51, 60,
   75, 102
Tolstoy, Leo, 152
Trentin, 76
Trotskyites, 129
Tupamaro Guerillas, 25

Ulam, Adam, 29
Union de la Gauche, 39, 46
Unità, 50, 52
United States, 138, 139,
   140
Uruguay, 20, 22, 25
USSR, 124, 137, 138, 139,
   143

Utopian socialists, 150

Vanguard Party, 31
Vargas, Getulio, 22
Vekhi group, 154
Venezuela, 22, 24, 33
Venezuela, Communist
   Party of, 24
Via Chilena, 24
Via Pacifica, 22, 24
Vietnam, 138
Void (polost'), 149
Vozhd, 51

Western Europe, 47
Wittfogel, Karl, 167
World War I, 151
World War II, 22

Yevtushenko, Yevgeni,
   161
Yugoslavia, 41, 42, 49,
   83